Brussels Travel guide 2024

Discover Brussels' Charms: A Contemporary Traveler's Handbook to the Vibrant Capital of Europe

By

Linda D. Ake

Table of Contents

Introduction

Overview of Brussels

Brussels, the vibrant capital of Belgium, stands as a testament to the country's rich history, cultural diversity, and political significance. Nestled in the heart of Europe, this cosmopolitan city serves as the de facto capital of the European Union, hosting key institutions that shape the continent's future.

As the capital of Belgium, Brussels seamlessly blends medieval charm with modern cosmopolitanism. Its historic architecture, picturesque squares, and lively neighborhoods create an enchanting backdrop for exploration. Beyond its national role, Brussels is a hub of international diplomacy, housing the European Commission, the Council of the European Union, and various other EU institutions.

Multicultural and Multilingual Character

One of Brussels' defining features is its multicultural and multilingual character. With French and Dutch as official languages, the city reflects the linguistic diversity that is a hallmark of Belgian identity. Visitors can immerse themselves in a tapestry of cultures, enjoying diverse cuisines, art, and traditions.

Whether you're drawn to the iconic Grand Place, intrigued by the surreal Atomium, or eager to explore the city's vibrant neighborhoods, Brussels promises a captivating experience that seamlessly marries tradition and modernity. Join us as we delve into the various facets of this dynamic city, uncovering its historical treasures, culinary delights, and the unique charm that sets Brussels apart.

Geography
Brussels is strategically situated in the central part of Belgium, serving as the de facto capital of both the country and the European Union. Its geographical coordinates are approximately 50.8503° N latitude and 4.3517° E longitude.

Topography
The topography of Brussels is relatively flat, with its elevation ranging from around 13 meters (43 feet) to 108 meters (354 feet) above sea level. The cityscape is characterized by a mix of historic architecture, modern buildings, and green spaces.

River and Waterways
The Senne River, once a more prominent feature of Brussels, has been largely covered over the years due to urbanization. Today, a network of canals, including the Brussels–Charleroi Canal, provides waterways through the city.

Green Spaces
Despite its urban setting, Brussels is known for its commitment to green spaces. Parks such as Parc du Cinquantenaire, Bois de la Cambre, and Josaphat Park offer residents and visitors serene areas to relax and enjoy nature.

Surrounding Regions
Brussels is centrally located within Belgium, making it well-connected to other major Belgian cities. It is approximately 173 kilometers (107 miles) southwest of Amsterdam, Netherlands, and about 173 kilometers (107 miles) northeast of Paris, France.

Climate
Brussels experiences a temperate maritime climate with mild summers and winters. Average temperatures range from around 3°C (37°F) in winter to 18°C (64°F) in summer. Rainfall is relatively evenly distributed throughout the year.

Urban Layout
The city is divided into various neighborhoods, each with its unique character. The historic city center, known for the UNESCO-listed Grand Place, contrasts with modern districts hosting EU institutions. The urban layout facilitates exploration

on foot, by bicycle, or by using the well-developed public transportation system.

Understanding the geographical context of Brussels enhances the appreciation of its diverse landscape, from historical landmarks to green oases, contributing to the city's dynamic and inviting atmosphere.

10 things to know before visiting

Comic Strip Murals
Brussels is known for its comic strip heritage. Take a stroll through the city to discover colorful murals depicting iconic comic book characters like Tintin, the Smurfs, and Asterix.

Art Nouveau Architecture
Brussels is a gem of Art Nouveau architecture. Explore neighborhoods like Ixelles and Saint-Gilles to admire the intricate designs of buildings created by renowned architect Victor Horta.

René Magritte's Surrealism
Belgium's famous surrealist painter, René Magritte, hails from Brussels. Visit the Magritte Museum to

explore his intriguing works, including "The Son of Man" and "The Treachery of Images."

Trappist Beers
Belgium is renowned for its beers, and some of the world's finest Trappist beers are brewed by monks in Belgian monasteries. Try unique and rich-flavored Trappist beers in Brussels' pubs and bars.

Smallest Statue: Manneken Pis
Witness the quirky charm of the Manneken Pis, a small bronze statue of a little boy urinating in a fountain. The statue has numerous costumes, and its attire is changed on various occasions and festivals.

Chocolate Workshops
Indulge your sweet tooth with Belgian chocolates, and take it a step further by participating in a chocolate-making workshop. Learn the art of chocolate crafting from local chocolatiers.

Music Instruments Museum
Explore the Museum of Musical Instruments, located in an Art Nouveau building. It houses a vast collection of musical instruments from around the world and offers panoramic views of the city from its rooftop.

Gastronomic Experiences

Experience Brussels' gastronomy through unusual dining options, such as dinner in the sky or meals served in unique settings. The city offers inventive and immersive culinary experiences.

Flower Carpet Festival

If visiting in August during even-numbered years, don't miss the Flower Carpet Festival at the Grand Place. The square is adorned with a stunning carpet made of colorful flowers, creating a spectacular display.

Language Surrealism

Embrace the linguistic surrealism of Brussels. Street signs, public notices, and official communications may be presented in both French and Dutch, sometimes leading to amusing language combinations.

These unique must-knows add an extra layer of charm and fascination to your visit to Brussels, ensuring a memorable and enriching experience.

Chapter 1:

Getting There

International Airports

Brussels is served by two major international airports: Brussels Airport (Zaventem) and Brussels South Charleroi Airport. Each airport has its own characteristics and serves as a gateway to the city and the broader region.

1.Brussels Airport (Zaventem) - BRU

Location: Distance from City Center: Approximately 12 kilometers (7.5 miles) northeast of Brussels city center.

Terminals:
Brussels Airport has one main terminal building divided into two piers: Pier A and Pier B.

Services and Facilities:
Airlines: Serves as a major hub for various international airlines.

Lounges: Offers lounges for different airlines and a Brussels Airlines lounge.

Shopping and Dining: Features a wide range of shops, restaurants, and cafes.

Transportation: Well-connected by train, bus, and taxi services to the city center.

Ground Transportation:
Train: The airport has its own train station, Brussels Airport-Zaventem, with direct connections to Brussels Central Station and other major cities.

Bus: Several bus lines connect the airport to different parts of Brussels and neighboring cities.

Taxi and Car Rental: Taxi and car rental services are readily available at the airport.

Parking:
Offers short-term and long-term parking options with various facilities.

Special Features:
Diamond Lounges: Exclusive lounges for premium passengers and frequent flyers.

Art and Culture: Exhibits and displays showcasing Belgian art and culture throughout the airport.

2.Brussels South Charleroi Airport - CRL
Location:
Distance from City Center: Approximately 46 kilometers (29 miles) south of Brussels city center.

Terminals:
Charleroi Airport has one terminal building serving both arrivals and departures.

Services and Facilities:
Airlines: Primarily used by low-cost carriers such as Ryanair.

Shopping and Dining: Provides a selection of shops and eateries.

VIP Lounge: Offers a VIP lounge for passengers seeking premium services.

Ground Transportation:
Bus: Direct shuttle services connect the airport to Brussels South Station.

Taxi and Car Rental: Taxi and car rental services are available at the airport.

Parking:
Offers convenient parking facilities for short-term and long-term stays.

Special Features:

Charleroi Adventure Airport (CAA): A dedicated area for families and children with games, play zones, and child-friendly facilities.

Both airports cater to different traveler preferences, with Brussels Airport being the primary international gateway and Brussels South Charleroi Airport offering cost-effective options, particularly for budget airlines.

Travelers can choose the airport that best suits their needs and travel plans.

Transportation Options

Brussels offers a diverse range of transportation options, making it convenient for visitors to explore the city and its surroundings.

Here are the key transportation modes in Brussels:

Public Transportation:

Metro:
- **Description:** Brussels has a well-developed metro system with four lines (1, 2, 5, and 6) that connect various parts of the city.

- **Advantages:** Fast and efficient, especially for navigating the city center.

Trams:
- **Description:** Extensive tram network covering different neighborhoods, offering a scenic way to explore the city.

- **Advantages:** Trams provide a comfortable means of transportation and are particularly useful for reaching areas not served by the metro.

Buses:
- **Description:** Comprehensive bus network connecting the city and suburbs.

- **Advantages:** Buses are a flexible option for reaching destinations not covered by the metro or tram lines.

Public Transportation Passes:
- **Description:** Integrated travel passes (STIB/MIVB) allow unlimited travel on buses, trams, and the metro for a specified duration.

- **Advantages:** Cost-effective for those planning to use public transportation frequently.

Bike Rentals:
- **Description:** Brussels promotes cycling, and bike rental services are available throughout the city.

- **Advantages:** Ideal for exploring the city at a leisurely pace, especially in areas with dedicated bike lanes.

Villo! Bike Share:
- **Description:** Villo! is Brussels' bike-sharing program with numerous stations across the city.

- **Advantages:** Convenient for short rides, and the first 30 minutes are often free with a subscription.

Taxis:

Taxi Stands:
- **Description:** Taxis are readily available at designated stands and can also be hailed on the street.

- **Advantages:** Comfortable and convenient, especially for reaching destinations not easily accessible by public transportation.

Car Rentals:

Car Rental Agencies:
- **Description:** Various car rental agencies operate in Brussels for those who prefer the flexibility of driving.

- **Advantages:** Useful for day trips or exploring areas outside the city center.

Train Services:

Train Stations:
- **Description:** Brussels is well-connected by train, with three major train stations: Brussels Central, Brussels Midi, and Brussels Nord.

- **Advantages:** Trains provide efficient intercity and international travel options.

Airport Shuttles:
- **Description:** Shuttle services connect the city center with Brussels Airport and Brussels South Charleroi Airport.

- **Advantages:** Convenient for airport transfers, with scheduled departures.

Understanding the variety of transportation options in Brussels empowers visitors to choose the most suitable means based on their preferences, schedules, and destinations. Whether exploring historical landmarks, navigating neighborhoods, or venturing beyond the city limits, Brussels provides a well-connected and accessible transportation network.

Navigating Public Transportation

Brussels boasts an efficient and well-connected public transportation system, comprising metro, trams, and buses, making it easy for visitors to explore the city and its diverse neighborhoods. Here's a comprehensive guide on how to navigate Brussels' public transportation:

Metro System:
Description: The Brussels Metro consists of four lines (1, 2, 5, and 6) that cover key areas of the city, including the European Quarter, city center, and suburbs.

Ticketing: Purchase single tickets or multi-day passes at metro stations or use contactless cards like MOBIB for seamless travel.

Frequency: Trains run frequently, especially during peak hours, and are a quick and reliable means of transportation.

Accessibility: Stations are equipped with elevators and escalators, making the metro accessible for passengers with mobility challenges.

Tram Network:
Description: Brussels has an extensive tram network connecting various neighborhoods, offering a scenic way to explore the city.

Routes: Trams cover both central and suburban areas, providing a comprehensive view of Brussels' urban landscape.

Ticket Integration: Use the same tickets and passes valid for the metro system for tram travel.

Travel Tips: Trams are an excellent choice for reaching destinations not served by the metro.

Bus Services:
Description: Buses complement the metro and tram network, serving areas not covered by rail transportation.

Routes: Extensive bus routes connect the city center to the suburbs and outskirts, offering flexibility in travel.

Tickets: Purchase tickets from the driver or use integrated travel passes for bus journeys.

Night Buses: Night buses operate after the metro and tram services conclude, providing transportation during late hours.

Integrated Travel Passes:
Description: STIB/MIVB offers integrated travel passes, allowing unlimited travel on buses, trams, and the metro for a specified duration.

Types: Options include single-journey tickets, day passes, and monthly or annual subscriptions.

Accessibility: Purchase and recharge these passes at kiosks, online, or at designated points throughout the city.

Navigational Apps:
Apps: Utilize mobile apps like STIB/MIVB official app or Google Maps for real-time information on schedules, routes, and delays.

User-Friendly: These apps assist in planning routes, estimating travel times, and locating the nearest transportation options.

Biking and Walking:
Bike Rentals: Brussels promotes cycling, and visitors can explore the city at their own pace using bike rental services.

Walking Routes: Many attractions are within walking distance of the city center, providing an opportunity to discover Brussels on foot.

Accessibility and Assistance:
Information Points: Find information points at major metro stations and key transit hubs for assistance.

Language: English is widely spoken, and transport staff help guide passengers.

Navigating public transportation in Brussels is an enriching experience that allows visitors to delve into the city's diverse neighborhoods while appreciating its efficient and interconnected transit system. Armed with this knowledge, travelers can confidently explore Brussels, whether they're heading to iconic landmarks, trendy neighborhoods, or hidden gems.

Chapter 2:

Accommodation

Budget Accommodation

Recommendations for Popular Hostels

Hey there! If you're planning a trip to Brussels on a budget, you'll be glad to know that the city offers plenty of affordable hostel accommodation options. From centrally located hostels with a social atmosphere to budget-friendly dormitory-style accommodations, there's something for everyone. Let me tell you about some of the best hostels in the city.

First up is Sleep Well Hostel, which is centrally located near the Grand Place. It offers affordable dormitory-style accommodations and modern facilities. The hostel is known for its vibrant atmosphere and social events, making it the perfect place to meet fellow travelers.

Next, we have MEININGER Brussels City Center, which is conveniently located close to transport links, providing easy access to the city center. This hostel combines hostel affordability with hotel-like facilities and offers a variety of room options, including private and shared rooms.

If you're looking for a budget-friendly option with a central location, Brussels 2GO4 Quality Hostel Grand Place is a great choice. It provides a mix of private and shared rooms and is known for its affordability and proximity to major attractions.

Brussels Hello Hostel is another lively option with a social atmosphere, located within walking distance of popular attractions. The hostel offers budget-friendly dormitory-style accommodations and is ideal for solo travelers and those looking to meet fellow guests.

For those interested in sustainability, Jacques Brel Youth Hostel is a great option. It's located in the heart of Brussels and offers budget-friendly dormitory-style accommodations with a focus on sustainability. The hostel also provides a friendly and communal environment.

Brussels 2GO4 Hostel Botanique is situated near the Botanique cultural complex and offers budget-friendly accommodations with a mix of private and shared rooms. It's also close to public transportation, making it easy to explore the city.

Hostel Grand Place is a centrally located hostel with a variety of room options. It's known for its friendly staff and sociable atmosphere, making it the perfect place to meet new people.

If you're looking for a budget-friendly option close to Brussels Midi/Zuid Station, MEININGER Hotel Brussels Gare du Midi is a great choice. It offers both private and shared rooms and focuses on comfort and convenience.

Brussels Youth Hostel is located near the Atomium and Mini-Europe and offers affordable dormitory-style accommodations. It's a great option for those exploring the Atomium and surrounding areas.

Finally, Generation Europe Youth Hostel is situated in the European Quarter and offers a diverse range of room options. It's ideal for travelers interested in EU institutions and nearby attractions.

All of these hostels cater to different preferences and offer a mix of central locations, social atmospheres, and budget-friendly accommodations, ensuring a diverse range of options for travelers exploring Brussels on a budget. So, take your pick and enjoy your stay in Brussels!

Guesthouses

Looking for affordable and comfortable accommodations for your Brussels trip? Check out the city's guesthouses, which offer a variety of options to meet your needs.

The Brussels Guesthouse, located in the Ixelles district, offers affordable rooms with a homely atmosphere, perfect for travelers seeking a cozy stay. B&B Urban Rooms, situated near public transportation, provides guests with modern amenities and a welcoming environment.

For those looking for a central location, The Opera Residence offers a variety of room options, making it an ideal choice for convenience and comfort. Alternatively, Le Valduc, nestled in Woluwe-Saint-Lambert, provides a peaceful escape with its tranquil garden and cozy rooms.

La Villa Zarin, located in the Saint-Gilles neighborhood, is known for its warm hospitality and affordable, comfortable rooms, making it an excellent choice for a homely stay. B&B Un Jardin en Ville, situated near public transportation, offers a peaceful retreat with its garden setting.

Guesthouse Maison Az, also located near public transportation, boasts unique decor and a welcoming ambiance with a mix of private and shared rooms. Le Lys d'Or, located in the Saint-Gilles neighborhood, offers budget-friendly accommodations with a friendly and welcoming atmosphere.

Lastly, B&B Villa 36, located near public transportation, offers an affordable and comfortable stay with a unique atmosphere.

In summary, these guesthouses offer a range of options for budget-conscious travelers and provide affordable, comfortable, and often unique stays in Brussels.

Affordable and Charming Options
Please find below the list of accommodations in Brussels that combine affordability with charm, making them suitable for travelers looking for a comfortable and distinctive experience without breaking the bank:

1. Sleep Well Hostel: Centrally located near the Grand Place, offering affordable dormitory-style accommodation. Known for its vibrant atmosphere and social events.

2. Brussels 2GO4 Quality Hostel Grand Place: Budget-friendly with a central location close to the

Grand Place. Provides a mix of private and shared rooms, combining affordability with charm.

3. Brussels Guesthouse: Situated in the Ixelles district, offering affordable rooms with a homely atmosphere. Perfect for those seeking a charming and intimate stay.

4. B&B Urban Rooms: A budget-friendly bed and breakfast with modern amenities, providing a cozy and welcoming environment. Located near public transportation for convenience.

5. Vintage Hotel Brussels: A boutique hotel near Avenue Louise, that combines affordability with a stylish retro design. A charming option for a unique stay.

6. Hotel Retro: Boutique hotel with a retro vibe, offering reasonably priced rooms and a unique design. Located near the European Quarter.

7. Le Valduc: Charming bed and breakfast with a garden in Woluwe-Saint-Lambert, providing a tranquil and affordable escape with a homely atmosphere.

8. La Villa Zarin: Cozy guesthouse with a homely atmosphere, offering affordable and comfortable rooms. Located in the Saint-Gilles neighborhood.

9. B&B Un Jardin en Ville: Affordable guesthouse with a garden setting, providing a peaceful retreat. Conveniently situated near public transportation.

10. Brussels Hello Hostel: Lively hotels within walking distance of popular attractions. Known for its social atmosphere, offering budget-friendly dormitory-style accommodations.

Mid-Range Accommodation
If you're planning a trip to Brussels and looking for accommodation that is not too expensive, but still comfortable and stylish, then you might want to consider these mid-range options.

For those who prefer boutique hotels, you can check out Hotel Made in Louise and Jam Hotel. The former is known for its elegant rooms and personalized service, while the latter is famous for its trendy design and vibrant atmosphere.

If bed and breakfasts are more your style, then you might want to take a look at B&B L'Art de la Fugue and B&B Côté Décor. The former offers stylish and cozy rooms, while the latter is located in a historic house and boasts unique decor.

For those who prefer the convenience of a hotel, Hotel Floris Arlequin Grand-Place and Pillows Grand Boutique Hotel Place Rouppe are excellent options. The former is centrally located near the Grand Place and offers modern amenities at an affordable price. The latter combines historic charm with modern amenities and provides a luxurious and comfortable stay.

If you're looking for serviced apartments, Aparthotel Adagio Brussels Grand Place and B-aparthotel Grand Place are great choices. The former provides modern apartments with kitchen facilities, ideal for extended stays, while the latter has luxury serviced apartments with contemporary design and a home-like atmosphere.

Finally, for those who want to stay in a trendy hotel, you might want to check out The Augustin, which offers chic rooms and a sophisticated atmosphere. Or you can try Vintage Hotel Brussels, a retro-inspired boutique hotel with unique decor.

These mid-range options cater to travelers looking for a balance between affordability and a more refined stay. Each accommodation provides a comfortable and stylish experience in Brussels, so you can choose the one that suits your preferences and budget.

Boutique Hotels

Brussels boasts a range of boutique hotels that offer unique and personalized experiences, each with a touch of charm and style. These hotels are known for their carefully curated design elements, personalized service, and attention to detail.

Hotel Made in Louise, located in the Ixelles neighborhood, is a stylish boutique hotel that features individually decorated rooms and an elegant design, providing a warm and welcoming atmosphere.

Jam Hotel, located in Saint-Gilles, is a trendy boutique hotel with a modern design and a vibrant atmosphere. It features comfortable rooms, and a rooftop terrace, and is a popular choice for guests who prefer a lively and energetic setting.

Vintage Hotel Brussels, located near Avenue Louise, is a retro-inspired boutique hotel that offers affordability and style. It features unique decor and a comfortable stay.

Hotel Amigo, located in the City Center near the Grand Place, is a luxury boutique hotel known for its elegant rooms, fine dining, and top-notch service.

The Dominican, a contemporary boutique hotel located in the city center, offers chic design, stylish rooms, and modern amenities.

Hotel Le Châtelain, situated in the upscale Ixelles neighborhood, is a sophisticated boutique hotel offering luxurious rooms and personalized service.

9Hotel Sablon is a stylish boutique hotel located in Sablon with a minimalist design and comfortable rooms, perfect for those seeking a central location near the Sablon district.

The Augustin, located near Avenue Louise, is a chic boutique hotel known for its trendy design, stylish rooms, and welcoming ambiance.

Hotel Manos Premier, located in Ixelles, is a boutique hotel that exudes a classic and luxurious atmosphere. It is known for its elegant decor, spacious rooms, and attentive service.

Finally, Hotel Pillows Grand Boutique Place Rouppe combines historic charm with modern amenities, providing guests with a luxurious and comfortable stay in the heart of Brussels.

These boutique hotels offer a unique and intimate atmosphere, perfect for those who want to experience the city in an exclusive and personalized way.

Unique and Stylish Choices
If you're looking for distinctive and stylish accommodations in Brussels, we have several unique options that may interest you.

The Pantone Hotel is a boutique hotel with vibrant and colorful decor inspired by the Pantone color system. It features modern rooms and a lively atmosphere.

The 9 Hotel Central is another boutique hotel with a contemporary and stylish design, which combines modern amenities with a unique touch. It is situated in the heart of the city, near the Grand Place.

The Vintage Hotel Brussels is also a boutique hotel, with retro-inspired decor, each room themed after a different music genre or artist. This trendy and unique experience is located near Avenue Louise.

Hotel Le Berger is a historic hotel with an artistic flair, celebrated for its unique and stylish interiors. It is located in the Ixelles district.

For those seeking an unforgettable stay, the Train Hostel offers creatively designed train carriages for accommodation.

Aloft Brussels Schuman is a trendy hotel that focuses on modern and trendy design, with a focus on technology and social spaces. It is located in the European Quarter, close to EU institutions.

The Dominican is a contemporary boutique hotel with a chic design and luxurious amenities. It is centrally located near major attractions.

9 Hotel Sablon is a boutique hotel with a minimalist design and a sophisticated atmosphere. It is situated in the heart of the Sablon district.

Finally, the Hotel Amigo is a luxury boutique hotel near the Grand Place, combining historic charm with elegant design and top-notch service.

These accommodations offer a mix of creative design, unique themes, and stylish interiors for travelers seeking a special and memorable touch in Brussels.

Bed and Breakfasts

Bed and breakfasts (B&Bs) in Brussels offer a cozy and often more intimate accommodation experience. Here are some recommendations for bed and breakfasts in the city:

B&B L'Art de la Fugue:

Location: Ixelles

Highlights: Stylish bed and breakfast with cozy rooms and a welcoming ambiance. Ideal for those looking for a personalized and intimate stay.

B&B Côté Décor:

Location: European Quarter

Highlights: Situated in a historic house, this bed and breakfast combines comfort with a unique decor. Close to European institutions.

B&B Urban Rooms:

Location: Near Public Transportation

Highlights: A budget-friendly bed and breakfast with modern amenities, providing a cozy and welcoming environment. Conveniently located for easy access to attractions.

B&B Un Jardin en Ville:

Location: Near Public Transportation

Highlights: An affordable guesthouse with a garden setting, offering a peaceful retreat close to the city center.

B&B Villa 36:

Location: Ixelles

Highlights: A charming bed and breakfast near public transportation, providing affordable and comfortable accommodations with a unique atmosphere.

B&B Les Taillis:

Location: Woluwe-Saint-Lambert

Highlights: Budget-friendly bed and breakfast offering a comfortable stay in a peaceful setting.

B&B Druum:

Location: City Center

Highlights: Centrally located bed and breakfast with modern amenities. Known for its friendly staff and comfortable accommodations.

Brussels Bed and Toast:

Location: Ixelles

Highlights: A budget-friendly guesthouse known for its friendly hosts and cozy atmosphere. Close to trendy shops and cafes.

Guesthouse Maison Az:

Location: Near Public Transportation

Highlights: A charming guesthouse with a mix of private and shared rooms. Known for its unique decor and welcoming ambiance.

B&B Salve:

Location: Near Public Transportation

Highlights: An affordable guesthouse offering a mix of private and shared rooms. Provides a comfortable and convenient stay for visitors.

These bed and breakfast options offer a range of atmospheres, from historic charm to modern comfort, providing travelers with a more personalized and home-like experience during their stay in Brussels.

Comfortable and Personalized Stays

The following is a compilation of select lodging options in Brussels, Belgium. These options include luxury boutique hotels, stylish bed and breakfasts, and accommodations with unique atmospheres. Among these, Hotel Amigo stands out as a luxury boutique hotel close to the Grand Place, which offers a charming combination of historic elegance and sophisticated design, coupled with top-notch service. Similarly, B&B L'Art de la Fugue is a stylish bed and breakfast located in Ixelles, which is ideal for a personalized and intimate stay. Another noteworthy option is 9Hotel Sablon, a minimalist boutique hotel in the Sablon district that offers a sophisticated and personalized atmosphere.

Hotel Le Châtelain, located in the upscale Ixelles neighborhood, is another sophisticated boutique hotel offering luxurious rooms and personalized service. Additionally, B&B Urban Rooms is a budget-friendly bed and breakfast that provides modern amenities and a welcoming environment. This accommodation is conveniently located near public transportation, making it an excellent option for those seeking easy access to attractions.

For those seeking a blend of historic charm and modern amenities, Hotel Pillows Grand Boutique Place Rouppe is a notable option located in the city center. Moreover, B&B Villa 36, situated in Ixelles, offers affordable and comfortable accommodations with a unique atmosphere, also near public transportation. The Dominican is a contemporary boutique hotel located in the city center near major attractions, boasting chic design and luxurious amenities. Finally, Le Valduc, located in Woluwe-Saint-Lambert, is a charming bed and breakfast with a garden, providing a tranquil and personalized escape. Jam Hotel, located in Saint-Gilles, is a trendy boutique hotel with a modern design that features comfortable rooms and a vibrant atmosphere.

Overall, these lodging options provide a diverse range of choices for travelers seeking a comfortable and personalized experience in Brussels.

Luxury Accommodation
5-Star Hotels
If you're looking for the ultimate luxury experience during your stay in Brussels, you'll find a wide range of high-end hotels that offer exquisite

amenities, superior service, and elegant surroundings. These luxurious accommodations are designed to cater to the most discerning travelers, who seek a refined and exclusive experience in Brussels. From historic hotels with opulent decor to modern establishments with panoramic views, each of these luxury hotels offers a unique experience.

If you're looking for a luxurious stay near the Grand Place, Hotel Amigo and Hotel de la Poste - Relais de Napoleon III are some excellent choices. Hotel Amigo is a luxurious 5-star hotel known for its elegant rooms, fine dining, and top-notch service, while Hotel de la Poste - Relais de Napoleon III is a historic luxury hotel with upscale rooms and personalized service.

For a modern and stylish luxury hotel with panoramic views of the city, The Hotel Brussels is an excellent choice. This hotel offers luxurious rooms, a spa, and Michelin-starred dining. Sofitel Brussels Le Louise is another 5-star hotel located on Avenue Louise that offers upscale rooms, a fitness center, and gourmet dining.

Steigenberger Wiltcher's is a luxury hotel situated on Avenue Louise that features lavish rooms, a spa, and a rooftop terrace with panoramic views. Warwick Brussels - Grand Place is another luxury hotel located near the Grand Place, offering elegant rooms, a rooftop terrace, and a fitness center.

Rocco Forte Hotel Amigo is a 5-star hotel with a prime location near the Grand Place. This hotel features luxurious accommodations, a spa, and fine dining. Martin's Château du Lac is located on the shores of Lake Genval and offers a tranquil setting, upscale rooms, and a gourmet restaurant.

If you're looking for a grand and historic luxury hotel, Hotel Le Plaza Brussels is an excellent choice. This hotel is located near the Botanique cultural complex and is known for its opulent decor and high-end amenities. Finally, Tangla Hotel Brussels is a luxury hotel with an Asian-inspired design, located near Woluwe Park. This hotel features spacious rooms, a spa, and gourmet dining.

Overall, these luxury accommodations offer the perfect blend of exceptional service, opulent surroundings, and convenient locations, making them ideal for travelers seeking the ultimate luxury experience during their stay in Brussels.

Opulent Choices with Premium Amenities

If you're planning a luxurious stay in Brussels, there are several opulent options to choose from. These hotels offer a combination of lavish accommodations, upscale amenities, and impeccable service, ensuring a memorable experience. Here are some of the best choices to consider:

One such option is Hotel Amigo, a 5-star luxury hotel located near the Grand Place. This hotel boasts opulent rooms, fine dining options, and top-notch service.

If you're looking for a modern and stylish luxury hotel, The Hotel Brussels is a great choice. With panoramic city views, upscale rooms, a spa, and Michelin-starred dining, this hotel offers a luxurious experience.

Another option is Sofitel Brussels Le Louise, situated on Avenue Louise. This 5-star hotel features luxurious rooms, a fitness center, gourmet dining, and a sophisticated ambiance.

For a luxurious stay on Avenue Louise, consider Steigenberger Wiltcher's. This hotel offers lavish rooms, a spa, and a rooftop terrace with stunning views.

Rocco Forte Hotel Amigo, another 5-star hotel near the Grand Place, is known for its luxurious accommodations, spa facilities, and high-end dining experience.

If you want to stay near the Grand Place, Warwick Brussels - Grand Place is a luxury hotel with elegant rooms, a rooftop terrace, and premium amenities for a luxurious stay.

If you're looking for a serene environment, Martin's Château du Lac is a luxurious hotel situated on the shores of Lake Genval. This hotel offers upscale rooms, a gourmet restaurant, and a beautiful setting.

Hotel Le Plaza Brussels is a grand and historic luxury hotel near the Botanique cultural complex. This hotel features opulent decor and high-end amenities.

Tangla Hotel Brussels is a luxury hotel with an Asian-inspired design, spacious rooms, a spa, and gourmet dining near Woluwe Park.

Finally, Steigenberger Grandhotel Brussels is a centrally located luxury hotel with sophisticated rooms, a wellness center, and excellent dining options.

These luxurious options offer a blend of comfort, luxury, and premium amenities, ensuring a memorable and opulent stay in Brussels.

Luxury Apartments

If you are seeking elegant and luxurious accommodation in Brussels for a longer and more private trip, there are several options available that provide premium amenities and top-notch services. These lavish apartments offer a unique and comfortable living experience that caters to the needs of discerning travelers. Here are some of the top recommendations that you may consider:

Aparthotel Adagio Brussels Grand Place: This modern serviced apartment is conveniently located near major attractions such as the Grand Place. It features well-equipped kitchens that make it easy for you to prepare your meals and enjoy a home-like atmosphere.

B-aparthotel Grand Place: This luxury serviced apartment is elegantly designed with contemporary furnishings and is close to major landmarks. It offers a comfortable and cozy living space that makes you feel like you are at home.

MAS Residence: This elegant serviced apartment is situated in the European Quarter and offers spacious and well-furnished units with modern amenities. It is perfect for travelers who want to feel at home while indulging in luxury living.

Smartflats Design - Grand Place: This stylish and fully equipped apartment is located near the Grand Place and offers a high level of comfort and convenience. It is ideal for both business and leisure travelers who are seeking a luxurious and comfortable place to stay.

Martin's Brussels EU: This modern apartment is located in the European Quarter and features fully equipped kitchens and a fitness center. It is ideal for an extended stay and offers a comprehensive living experience.

Aparthotel Citadines Toison d'Or Brussels: This luxury apartment is designed with contemporary furnishings and is located near Avenue Louise. It offers a comfortable and convenient stay for travelers who want to indulge in luxury living.

Residence Palace: This spacious and well-appointed apartment is situated in a central location and offers a premium living experience. It is perfect for travelers who want to enjoy a luxurious and comfortable stay in Brussels.

Smartflats Design - Berlaymont: This luxury apartment is located in the European Quarter and features a sleek and modern design. It is well-suited for both business and leisure travelers who want to enjoy a luxurious and comfortable stay.

Brussels Central Flats: This elegant apartment is situated in the heart of Brussels and offers fully equipped kitchens and stylish interiors. It is perfect for travelers who want to enjoy a luxurious and comfortable stay in the city center.

The Dominican Residence: This luxurious serviced apartment is situated in a central location and provides a comfortable and upscale living environment. It is perfect for travelers who want to indulge in luxury living while enjoying the convenience of a central location in Brussels.

Exclusive and Spacious Living
If you're on the lookout for spacious and exclusive living options in Brussels, you'll be pleased to know that there are upscale residences and serviced apartments that offer luxurious amenities and ample space. Here are some recommendations for those who prioritize comfort and sophistication during their stay in Brussels:

Catalonia Grand Place
This elegant serviced apartment, with a central location, provides spacious living areas and premium amenities.

Brussels Exclusive Apartments
This is a collection of exclusive and spacious apartments in various central locations, offering high-end furnishings and services.

Sweet Inn
Luxury apartments with stylish interiors, located in prime neighborhoods, offer a personalized and exclusive living experience.

B-aparthotel Montgomery
This is a spacious and well-designed serviced apartment near Montgomery Square, providing a comfortable and exclusive atmosphere.

MAS Residence
Elegant serviced apartments in the European Quarter, are known for their spacious layouts and sophisticated design.

Aparthotel Citadines Toison d'Or Brussels
Luxury apartments with contemporary design, offering spacious living areas near Avenue Louise.

Martin's Brussels EU
Modern apartments in the European Quarter, featuring fully equipped kitchens and generous living spaces.

Smartflats Design - Berlaymont
Exclusive serviced apartments in the European Quarter, are known for their sleek design and spacious interiors.

Brussels Central Flats
Elegant apartments in the heart of Brussels, provide a combination of style and spacious living.

Residence Palace
Spacious and well-appointed apartments in a central location, offering exclusive living arrangements.

These options provide a combination of luxury, exclusivity, and generous living spaces, making them ideal for those who are seeking a comfortable and sophisticated living experience in Brussels.

Unique Accommodation
Historic Inns
While Brussels is known for its historic charm, traditional inns, in the classic sense, might be less common compared to other types of accommodations. However, some historic hotels

and establishments offer a glimpse into the city's rich past. Here are some options that capture a sense of history in Brussels:

Hotel Amigo:
Highlights: A luxury hotel located near the Grand Place, known for its historic charm and association with famous guests. The hotel has retained elements of its past while providing modern amenities.

Hotel Métropole:
Highlights: Established in 1895, Hotel Métropole is one of Brussels' oldest hotels. It features a historic and opulent interior, offering a glimpse into the city's belle époque era.

Royal Windsor Hotel Grand Place:
Highlights: Situated near the Grand Place, this hotel combines modern luxury with a historic setting. The building itself has a storied history, and its interior reflects a sense of tradition.

Hotel Le Plaza Brussels:
Highlights: A grand hotel that dates back to the 1930s, Hotel Le Plaza features Art Deco architecture and a rich history. It offers a blend of historic elegance and contemporary comfort.

Warwick Brussels - Grand Place:
Highlights: Located near the Grand Place, this hotel occupies a 19th-century building. It preserves elements of its historic character while providing upscale accommodations.

While the term "inn" might not be as commonly used in Brussels, these historic hotels provide a sense of tradition, allowing guests to immerse themselves in the city's cultural and architectural heritage. Each of these establishments combines historical elements with modern amenities for a unique and enriching stay.

Stay in Elegance with a Historical Touch
If you're seeking accommodations that blend elegance with a historical touch in Brussels, several establishments offer a luxurious experience within a historical setting. Here are some recommendations:

Hotel Amigo:
Highlights: A luxury hotel near the Grand Place, Hotel Amigo combines historical charm with modern luxury. It is known for its association with famous guests and its elegant ambiance.

Hotel Métropole:
Highlights: Dating back to 1895, Hotel Métropole is one of Brussels' oldest hotels. It features opulent decor, a historic atmosphere, and a central location.

Royal Windsor Hotel Grand Place:

Highlights: Situated near the Grand Place, this hotel offers a blend of historical charm and modern comfort. The building has a rich history, and the interior reflects a sense of tradition.

Hotel Le Plaza Brussels:

Highlights: An Art Deco gem from the 1930s, Hotel Le Plaza Brussels exudes historical elegance. It offers luxurious accommodations with a touch of grandeur.

Warwick Brussels - Grand Place:

Highlights: Occupying a 19th-century building near the Grand Place, Warwick Brussels maintains its historical character while providing upscale amenities and services.

Amigo Art Hotel:

Highlights: Nestled in the heart of Brussels, this boutique hotel offers a blend of art, history, and elegance, providing a unique and sophisticated stay.

Steigenberger Wiltcher's:

Highlights: Located on Avenue Louise, this luxurious hotel is housed in a historic building, offering a perfect combination of heritage and modern luxury.

Hotel des Galeries:
Highlights: Set in a building dating back to the 19th century, this boutique hotel near the Grand Place features elegant design and a historical ambiance.

Hotel Le Dixseptième:
Highlights: Situated in a 17th-century building, this boutique hotel offers period charm with modern amenities, providing an intimate and elegant atmosphere.

Sofitel Brussels Le Louise:
Highlights: This 5-star hotel on Avenue Louise combines contemporary luxury with a historical touch, providing a sophisticated and elegant stay.

These options ensure that guests experience the historical richness of Brussels while enjoying the comforts and elegance of upscale accommodations. Whether it's Art Deco, Belle Époque, or a 17th-century setting, these hotels offer a unique blend of history and luxury.

Eco-Friendly Stays
For travelers seeking eco-friendly stays in Brussels, some accommodations prioritize sustainability and environmental responsibility. Here are some options for eco-conscious stays in the city:

Tangla Hotel Brussels:
Eco-Friendly Features: This hotel is committed to sustainable practices, including energy-efficient lighting, waste reduction, and eco-friendly amenities.

Thon Hotel EU:
Eco-Friendly Features: Thon Hotel EU emphasizes sustainability with eco-certified rooms, energy-saving initiatives, and a focus on reducing environmental impact.

Martin's Klooster:
Eco-Friendly Features: Set in a former monastery, Martin's Klooster implements eco-friendly practices, including waste reduction and energy-efficient measures.

Aparthotel Adagio Brussels Grand Place:
Eco-Friendly Features: Adagio Brussels Grand Place is committed to sustainable tourism, with efforts in waste reduction, water conservation, and eco-friendly amenities.

Pantone Hotel:
Eco-Friendly Features: The Pantone Hotel emphasizes sustainable practices and features eco-friendly materials in its design and operations.

Jam Hotel:
Eco-Friendly Features: Jam Hotel incorporates eco-friendly initiatives, including energy-efficient lighting and a commitment to responsible tourism.

Hilton Brussels Grand Place:
Eco-Friendly Features: Hilton Brussels Grand Place implements sustainability measures, including waste reduction and energy efficiency, as part of its commitment to environmental responsibility.

Hotel Le Plaza Brussels:
Eco-Friendly Features: Hotel Le Plaza Brussels is committed to sustainable practices, including energy-saving measures and waste reduction initiatives.

MEININGER Brussels City Center:
Eco-Friendly Features: MEININGER incorporates eco-friendly measures in its operations, such as energy-efficient lighting and waste reduction.

9Hotel Sablon:
Eco-Friendly Features: 9Hotel Sablon is committed to environmental responsibility and implements eco-friendly practices in its daily operations.

These accommodations are dedicated to minimizing their environmental impact and providing eco-conscious travelers with sustainable and responsible lodging options in Brussels. It's always a good idea to check with the hotels directly about their specific eco-friendly initiatives and certifications.

Environmentally Conscious Accommodations.
For environmentally-conscious travelers, Brussels offers accommodations that prioritize sustainability and eco-friendly practices. Here are some options for environmentally conscious stays in the city:

Tangla Hotel Brussels:
Eco-Friendly Features: Tangla Hotel emphasizes sustainability with energy-efficient lighting, waste reduction, and eco-friendly amenities.

Thon Hotel EU:
Eco-Friendly Features: Thon Hotel EU is committed to sustainability with eco-certified rooms, energy-saving initiatives, and a focus on reducing environmental impact.

Martin's Klooster:
Eco-Friendly Features: Set in a former monastery, Martin's Klooster implements eco-friendly practices, including waste reduction and energy-efficient measures.

Aparthotel Adagio Brussels Grand Place:
Eco-Friendly Features: Adagio Brussels Grand Place is committed to sustainable tourism, with efforts in waste reduction, water conservation, and eco-friendly amenities.

Pantone Hotel:
Eco-Friendly Features: The Pantone Hotel emphasizes sustainable practices and features eco-friendly materials in its design and operations.

Jam Hotel:
Eco-Friendly Features: Jam Hotel incorporates eco-friendly initiatives, including energy-efficient lighting and a commitment to responsible tourism.

Hilton Brussels Grand Place:
Eco-Friendly Features: Hilton Brussels Grand Place implements sustainability measures, including waste reduction and energy efficiency, as part of its commitment to environmental responsibility.

Hotel Le Plaza Brussels:
Eco-Friendly Features: Hotel Le Plaza Brussels is committed to sustainable practices, including energy-saving measures and waste reduction initiatives.

MEININGER Brussels City Center:
Eco-Friendly Features: MEININGER incorporates eco-friendly measures in its operations, such as energy-efficient lighting and waste reduction.

9Hotel Sablon:
Eco-Friendly Features: 9Hotel Sablon is committed to environmental responsibility and implements eco-friendly practices in its daily operations.

These accommodations prioritize environmental sustainability, offering eco-conscious travelers the opportunity to stay in establishments that share their commitment to responsible tourism. Always check with the hotels directly to inquire about their specific eco-friendly initiatives and certifications.

Recommended Neighborhoods
City Center
The City Center of Brussels, also known as the Historic Center or Central Brussels, is the heart of the Belgian capital and a UNESCO World Heritage site. It's a place where the old and the new come together to create a unique blend of history, culture, and architecture.

The central square, Grand Place, is surrounded by beautiful guild halls, the Town Hall, and the King's House. It's considered one of the most beautiful squares in the world, with stunning architecture, flower carpet events that happen every two years, and a lively atmosphere filled with cafes and events.

Near the Grand Place, you'll find the famous bronze statue of a little boy urinating, known as Manneken Pis. It's a symbol of the irreverent spirit of Brussels, and it wears different costumes several times a week to reflect different themes and events.

One of the oldest shopping galleries in Europe, the Saint-Hubert Royal Galleries, is known for its elegant architecture and high-end shops. It's a charming covered arcade that houses luxury boutiques, chocolate shops, theaters, and cafes.

The Cathedral of St. Michael and St. Gudula is a stunning Gothic cathedral, the national church of Belgium, known for its impressive architecture and beautiful stained glass windows. It features twin towers, a Baroque-style pulpit, and ornate chapels inside.

The Royal Palace of Brussels is the official palace of the Belgian King. While the interior is not regularly open to the public, the surrounding park is a pleasant place for a stroll.

The Mont des Arts is a beautifully landscaped area offering panoramic views of the city and hosting cultural institutions such as the Royal Library and the Magritte Museum. It's a garden setting with stunning views and artistic attractions.

The Brussels City Museum, located in the King's House on the Grand Place, showcases the history of Brussels through artifacts, paintings, and exhibits. It displays the history of the Grand Place, Manneken Pis, and the development of the city.

The City Center of Brussels is filled with a variety of eateries, from traditional Belgian brasseries to international cuisine. It's the perfect place to enjoy Belgian waffles, chocolates, and beers in the many cafes and restaurants around the Grand Place.

The Bourse is an impressive neoclassical building that was once the stock exchange of Brussels. It's known for its architectural grandeur and occasional events and exhibitions held within.

The City Center of Brussels is easily accessible by public transportation, including metro, buses, and trams. Many attractions are within walking distance, making it a must-visit for anyone exploring the Belgian capital.

Proximity to Major Attractions

The City Center of Brussels is strategically located, offering proximity to major attractions, historical landmarks, and cultural sites. This central area ensures that visitors have easy access to the city's most renowned points of interest. Here's a breakdown of the proximity of the City Center to major attractions:

Grand Place (Grote Markt):

Proximity: The Grand Place is at the heart of the City Center, making it easily accessible by foot from various points within the area.

Manneken Pis:

Proximity: Located near the Grand Place, Manneken Pis is a short walk away from the central square.

Saint-Hubert Royal Galleries (Galeries Royales Saint-Hubert):

Proximity: These elegant galleries are situated in the City Center, with easy access from the Grand Place.

Cathedral of St. Michael and St. Gudula:

Proximity: The cathedral is within walking distance from the Grand Place, situated to the northeast of the central square.

Royal Palace of Brussels:
Proximity: The Royal Palace is located just to the southeast of the City Center, within a reasonable walking distance from the Grand Place.

Mont des Arts:
Proximity: This landscaped area with cultural institutions is adjacent to the City Center, easily reachable on foot.

Brussels City Museum (Museum van de Stad Brussel):
Proximity: Housed in the King's House on the Grand Place, the museum is centrally located.

Restaurants and Cafes:
Proximity: The City Center is dotted with a wide range of eateries, offering culinary delights within easy reach of major attractions.

Bourse (Brussels Stock Exchange):
Proximity: The Bourse is located to the northwest of the Grand Place, and it's a short walk from the central square.

Accessibility:
Proximity: The City Center is well-connected by public transportation, including metro, buses, and

trams, providing easy access to attractions in and around Brussels.

The central location of the City Center ensures that visitors can explore Brussels' most iconic attractions on foot, allowing for a convenient and immersive experience in the heart of the city. Whether it's historic landmarks, cultural institutions, or culinary delights, the major attractions are within close reach in the bustling City Center.

Ixelles

Ixelles is a vibrant and diverse neighborhood in Brussels, known for its eclectic atmosphere, historic architecture, and lively cultural scene. Here's an overview of Ixelles:

Avenue Louise:

Description: One of Brussels' most upscale shopping streets, Avenue Louise runs through Ixelles. It is lined with high-end boutiques, designer stores, and luxury brands.

Flagey Square (Place Flagey):

Description: A central square that serves as a cultural hub in Ixelles. It's known for the iconic Flagey building, which houses a cultural center, a concert hall, and a variety of restaurants and cafes.

Ixelles Ponds (Étangs d'Ixelles):
Description: A series of interconnected ponds surrounded by green spaces, providing a peaceful retreat in the heart of Ixelles. It's a popular spot for leisurely walks and picnics.

Matongé:
Description: A lively district within Ixelles known for its African and international influences. Matongé offers a diverse range of shops, restaurants, and cultural experiences.

Flagey Building:
Description: An iconic Art Deco building in Flagey Square, it houses cultural spaces, a concert hall, and the Flagey Brasserie. It's a focal point for arts and entertainment.

Cemetery of Ixelles (Cimetière d'Ixelles):
Description: A historic cemetery with notable graves and monuments. It provides a serene environment for reflection and exploration.

Bois de la Cambre:
Description: A large public park on the southeastern edge of Ixelles, Bois de la Cambre offers walking paths, a lake, and recreational activities. It's a popular spot for outdoor enthusiasts.

Elsene/Ixelles Ponds & Abbey:
Description: The Ixelles Ponds and Abbey are picturesque spots surrounded by greenery. The Abbey of La Cambre, with its beautiful architecture, is a notable landmark in the area.

Université Libre de Bruxelles (ULB):
Description: One of the main French-speaking universities in Brussels, ULB has a campus in Ixelles. The university adds a youthful and academic vibe to the neighborhood.

Eateries and Cafes:
Description: Ixelles is known for its diverse culinary scene, with numerous cafes, bistros, and international restaurants offering a wide range of dining options.

Ixelles is a dynamic neighborhood that seamlessly blends the old and the new, attracting residents and visitors alike with its cultural richness, green spaces, and trendy ambiance. Whether you're interested in shopping on Avenue Louise, exploring cultural venues, or enjoying the tranquility of parks, Ixelles has something to offer everyone.

Trendy Neighborhood with Local Charm
Saint-Gilles
Bohemian Vibe and Artistic Community

Accommodation Booking Tips
Online Booking Platforms

Brussels offers a variety of accommodation options, and several online booking platforms can help you find and reserve the perfect place for your stay. Here are some popular online booking platforms widely used in Brussels:

Booking.com:

Description: One of the most popular online travel agencies worldwide, Booking.com offers a vast selection of hotels, hostels, apartments, and other accommodation options in Brussels. The platform provides user reviews, detailed property information, and flexible booking options.

Expedia:

Description: Expedia is a comprehensive travel platform that allows users to book flights, hotels, car rentals, and vacation packages. It offers a wide range of accommodation choices in Brussels, along with customer reviews and loyalty program benefits.

Hotels.com:

Description: Hotels.com specializes in hotel bookings and provides a variety of options in Brussels. The platform offers a loyalty program where users can earn free nights for every ten nights booked.

Airbnb:
Description: Airbnb is a popular platform for booking private accommodations, including apartments, houses, and unique stays. In Brussels, you can find a diverse range of options, from centrally located apartments to charming local homes.

Agoda:
Description: Agoda is known for its extensive coverage in the Asia-Pacific region but also offers a wide selection of accommodations globally. It provides user reviews and deals on hotels, hostels, and more in Brussels.

Trivago:
Description: Trivago compares hotel prices from various booking sites, helping users find the best deals. It aggregates information from different platforms, allowing you to make an informed decision on accommodation in Brussels.

Hostelworld:
Description: If you're looking for budget-friendly options like hostels, Hostelworld is a go-to platform. It specializes in hostel bookings and

provides user reviews and ratings to help you choose the right one for your stay.

Kayak:
Description: Kayak is a comprehensive travel search engine that allows users to find and compare prices for flights, hotels, and rental cars. It aggregates information from various platforms, making it a useful tool for finding accommodation in Brussels.

Priceline:
Description: Priceline offers a range of travel services, including hotel bookings. The platform allows users to bid on hotel rooms or choose from published deals, providing potential savings on accommodations in Brussels.

HomeAway:
Description: HomeAway is a vacation rental platform that lists entire homes and apartments. It's an excellent option if you prefer a more home-like experience during your stay in Brussels.

Before booking, make sure to read reviews, check cancellation policies, and compare prices across different platforms to secure the best deal for your preferred accommodation in Brussels.

Popular Websites for Accommodation

To find accommodation in Brussels, you can explore several popular websites that offer a variety of options ranging from hotels and hostels to apartments and vacation rentals. Here are some popular websites for accommodation in Brussels:

Booking.com:

Description: Booking.com is a widely used platform offering a diverse range of accommodation options in Brussels. It provides detailed property information, user reviews, and flexible booking options.

Expedia:

Description: Expedia is a comprehensive travel platform where you can book hotels, flights, car rentals, and vacation packages. It features a variety of accommodation choices in Brussels with customer reviews and loyalty program benefits.

Hotels.com:

Description: Hotels.com specializes in hotel bookings and provides a wide selection of options in Brussels. The platform offers a loyalty program where users can earn free nights for every ten nights booked.

Airbnb:

Description: Airbnb is a popular platform for booking private accommodations, including apartments, houses, and unique stays. In Brussels, you can find a diverse range of options, from centrally located apartments to charming local homes.

Agoda:

Description: Agoda is known for its extensive coverage in the Asia-Pacific region and offers a variety of accommodations globally. It provides user reviews and deals on hotels, hostels, and more in Brussels.

Trivago:

Description: Trivago compares hotel prices from various booking sites, helping users find the best deals. It aggregates information from different platforms, allowing you to make an informed decision on accommodation in Brussels.

Hostelworld:

Description: If you're looking for budget-friendly options like hostels, Hostelworld is a specialized platform. It provides user reviews and ratings to help you choose the right hostel for your stay in Brussels.

Kayak:

Description: Kayak is a comprehensive travel search engine that allows users to find and compare prices for flights, hotels, and rental cars. It aggregates information from various platforms, making it a useful tool for finding accommodation in Brussels.

Priceline:

Description: Priceline offers a range of travel services, including hotel bookings. The platform allows users to bid on hotel rooms or choose from published deals, providing potential savings on accommodations in Brussels.

HomeAway:

Description: HomeAway is a vacation rental platform that lists entire homes and apartments. It's an excellent option if you prefer a more home-like experience during your stay in Brussels.

Before booking, consider your preferences, read reviews, and compare prices across different platforms to secure the best accommodation for your needs in Brussels.

Ways to Save on Accommodation Costs

Saving on accommodation costs is a smart way to stretch your travel budget. Here are several strategies to help you save on accommodation costs during your stay in Brussels or any other destination:

Book in Advance:
Advantage: Many hotels and accommodations offer lower rates for bookings made well in advance. Planning allows you to secure better deals.

Use Price Comparison Sites:
Advantage: Utilize platforms like Booking.com, Expedia, or Kayak to compare prices across various accommodation providers. This helps you find the best deals.

Consider Alternative Accommodations:
Advantage: Explore options beyond traditional hotels. Consider vacation rentals on Airbnb, HomeAway, or guesthouses for potentially lower costs and unique experiences.

Stay Outside the City Center:
Advantage: Accommodations in city centers are often more expensive. Look for options slightly outside the center with good transportation connections to save money.

Look for Package Deals:

Advantage: Some travel websites offer package deals that include both flights and accommodation. Bundling services can result in overall cost savings.

Check for Deals and Promotions:

Advantage: Keep an eye out for special promotions, discounts, or last-minute deals offered by hotels and booking platforms. Subscribe to newsletters for notifications.

Join Loyalty Programs:

Advantage: Loyalty programs offered by hotel chains or booking platforms often provide perks like discounts, free nights, or exclusive deals for members.

Flexible Dates and Off-Peak Travel:

Advantage: Being flexible with your travel dates can help you find lower rates. Off-peak seasons usually offer more affordable accommodation options.

Consider Hostels or Budget Hotels:

Advantage: Hostels and budget hotels often provide economical options for travelers. They can be an excellent choice for those on a tight budget.

Negotiate or Use Price Match Guarantees:
Advantage: Some hotels have price match guarantees. If you find a lower rate elsewhere, they may match or beat it. Negotiating directly with the hotel is also an option.

Book Refundable Rates:
Advantage: Opt for refundable rates when possible. While they may be slightly more expensive, they offer flexibility in case your plans change.

Consider Long-Term Stays:
Advantage: If your schedule allows, consider longer stays. Many accommodations offer discounted rates for extended bookings.

Stay with Locals:
Advantage: Platforms like Couchsurfing or house-sitting websites allow you to stay with locals for free or at a minimal cost, providing a unique cultural experience.

Use Travel Credit Cards:
Advantage: Some credit cards offer travel rewards, points, or cashback on accommodation expenses. Take advantage of these perks to reduce costs.

Ask for Discounts:
Advantage: When booking directly with a hotel, inquire about any available discounts such as AAA, military, or senior discounts.

By combining these strategies, you can significantly reduce your accommodation expenses and make your travel budget go further in Brussels or any other destination.

Chapter 3:

Attractions

Grand Place (Grote Markt)
Historical Significance:
Grand Place holds immense historical significance for Brussels. It has been the central market square since the 11th century, evolving to become a symbol of the city's prosperity and cultural heritage. The square witnessed various historical events, trade activities, and civic celebrations, making it a focal point for the people of Brussels.

Notable Buildings:
Guildhalls:
The square is surrounded by opulent guild halls, each showcasing unique architectural styles.

Historically, these guild halls represented different artisanal and trade guilds, contributing to the city's economic and social fabric.

Town Hall (Hôtel de Ville):
A Gothic masterpiece, the Town Hall stands as a testament to Brussels' political and administrative history.

Its tall spire, intricate facade, and grandeur make it a key landmark within Grand Place.

King's House (Maison du Roi):
Also known as the Breadhouse, the King's House is a prominent building that houses the Museum of the City of Brussels.
Its architecture adds to the overall charm of Grand Place, and it has been witness to various historical events.

Events and Festivals:
Grand Place is not only an architectural marvel but also a vibrant cultural space hosting numerous events and festivals. The square comes alive during events like the Flower Carpet, where intricate floral designs cover the ground, creating a breathtaking spectacle.

Illumination at Night:
In the evening, Grand Place is beautifully illuminated, creating a magical atmosphere. The illuminated guildhalls and Town Hall contribute to the square's enchanting nighttime ambiance, making it a must-visit during both day and night.

Restaurants and Cafes:
The square is surrounded by a plethora of restaurants and cafes, allowing visitors to enjoy

Belgian cuisine and waffles while soaking in the stunning architecture and lively atmosphere.

Grand Place remains an essential destination for locals and tourists alike, offering a blend of historical significance, architectural beauty, and cultural vibrancy. If you have any specific aspects you'd like to explore further, feel free to let me know!

4.1.1 Historical Significance
The historical significance of Grand Place (Grote Markt) in Brussels is profound, dating back to the 11th century. Here are key points highlighting the historical importance of this iconic square:

Medieval Origins:
Grand Place traces its origins to the medieval marketplace that emerged in the 11th century. Merchants and traders gathered in the square for commerce and exchange.

Marketplace Evolution:
Over the centuries, Grand Place evolved from a simple market square to a central hub for economic, social, and political activities in Brussels.

Role in Civic Life:

The square became the epicenter of civic life, witnessing events ranging from markets and fairs to civic ceremonies and celebrations.

Wealth and Prosperity:
During the Golden Age of Brussels in the 16th century, the city became a prosperous trading center. Grand Place became a symbol of this prosperity, and the guild halls constructed during this period reflected the wealth of the city's guilds.

Political Significance:
Grand Place played a crucial role in political events, serving as a venue for important declarations, celebrations, and even executions.

Destruction and Reconstruction:
In 1695, the square-faced destruction during the bombardment of Brussels by French troops. However, it was meticulously reconstructed, maintaining its historic layout and character.

UNESCO World Heritage Site:
In recognition of its historical and architectural significance, Grand Place was designated a UNESCO World Heritage Site in 1998. It is recognized as an outstanding example of a medieval square that has preserved its historic features.

Symbol of Brussels:
Grand Place stands as a symbol of Brussels' rich history, resilience, and cultural heritage. It encapsulates the spirit of the city and continues to be a focal point for both locals and visitors.

Grand Place's historical journey reflects the evolution of Brussels itself, from a medieval market square to a UNESCO-recognized gem that encapsulates the city's cultural, economic, and political legacy. The square remains a testament to the enduring spirit of Brussels across centuries.

4.1.2 Notable Buildings
Let's embark on a detailed exploration of the remarkable buildings surrounding the Grand Place (Grote Markt) in the beautiful city of Brussels. The square is surrounded by a series of opulent guild halls, each boasting unique and striking architectural features. These guild halls served as the meeting places for different artisanal and trade guilds, highlighting their economic and social significance in Brussels' history. The guildhalls exhibit a diverse range of architectural styles, including Gothic, Renaissance, and Baroque elements, adding to the grandeur and uniqueness of the Grand Place.

One of the most remarkable buildings located on the south side of the square is the Gothic masterpiece, the Town Hall (Hôtel de Ville). The Town Hall's tall spire, intricate sculptures, and detailed facade exemplify the Gothic architecture and symbolize Brussels' political power since the Middle Ages. It also serves as a venue for various official events, adding to its historical significance.

Another notable building is the King's House (Maison du Roi), also known as the Breadhouse, situated on the central square. The building's architecture is a blend of Gothic and Renaissance styles, creating an exquisite and grand appearance. It houses the Museum of the City of Brussels, displaying artifacts and exhibits related to the city's rich history.

The Dukes of Brabant's House (Maison des Ducs de Brabant), located on the eastern side of Grand Place, is another magnificent guildhall. Its facade is adorned with gilded statues, and the building showcases a mix of architectural styles, including Gothic and Baroque elements, adding to its overall grandeur.

The Guild of the Brewers (La Maison des Brasseurs) is recognized for its stunning facade featuring a large statue of St. Michael, the patron saint of Brussels. It represents the brewing guild's influence during Brussels' flourishing beer trade.

The Guild of the Archers (Les Arbalétriers), situated on the northwest corner of the square, features a distinctive facade with statues of archers. It represents the archers' guild, emphasizing the military and defensive history of Brussels.

Lastly, the Guild of the Tailors (La Maison des Tailleurs) is known for its elegant facade adorned with sculptures of tailors. The building reflects the prosperity and craftsmanship associated with the tailors' guild.

Together, these notable buildings form an aesthetically pleasing and historically rich architectural ensemble, making the Grand Place one of the most remarkable squares in Europe. The diversity of styles and the detailed craftsmanship in each building contribute to the unique character of this UNESCO World Heritage Site.

Manneken Pis

Manneken Pis is a famous statue located in Brussels that depicts a little boy urinating into a fountain. The statue is only 61 cm tall and is made of bronze.

It holds a lot of cultural significance for the city and has become a popular tourist attraction.

The statue has been around since the early 17th century, and the current bronze version was crafted during the same time. Manneken Pis has become a symbol of Brussels' humor and resilience. There are several legends surrounding the statue, including one where a little boy urinates on a bomb's fuse during an attack, saving the city.

One of the unique things about Manneken Pis is that it is dressed in different outfits donated by people and organizations. These outfits reflect the city's cultural events and celebrations. The changing of costumes is often tied to specific occasions, festivals, or commemorations, making the statue more festive and dynamic.

Manneken Pis is an active participant in cultural and civic events, and its attire can represent themes related to the event being celebrated. Despite its small size, the statue has gained global recognition and has become an iconic representation of Brussels' character.

The popularity of Manneken Pis has led to the creation of several replicas and similar statues, both within Brussels and in other parts of the world. The statue is not just a bronze figure, but a living symbol of Brussels' wit, resilience, and the city's ability to embrace its own unique and sometimes irreverent identity.

Atomium

The Atomium is an impressive architectural structure built as the main pavilion for the 1958 Brussels World's Fair. It comprises interconnected spheres that represent an iron crystal magnified 165 billion times. This design emphasizes the theme of the peaceful use of atomic energy and reflects a fascination with scientific progress and the potential for technological advancements in the post-war era.

The Atomium gained global attention and became a symbol of Belgium's optimism and technological advancement. After Expo 58, it became a permanent landmark in Brussels and one of the most visited attractions in Belgium, drawing tourists and locals alike.

The Atomium houses both temporary and permanent exhibitions inside its spheres, covering a range of topics related to science, technology, and the history of the Atomium itself. Exhibits provide educational content and showcase scientific progress, industry, and culture.

Royal Museums of Fine Arts of Belgium

The Royal Museums of Fine Arts of Belgium (Musées Royaux des Beaux-Arts de Belgique) is a complex of art museums in Brussels, housing an extensive collection of paintings, sculptures, and drawings. The museums are divided into two main parts: the Museum of Ancient Art and the Museum of Modern Art. Additionally, there are the Wiertz Museum and the Meunier Museum, which are part of the Royal Museums complex. Here's an overview:

Museum of Ancient Art:

Collection: This museum primarily focuses on European art from the 15th to the 18th centuries.

Highlights: It features works by renowned artists such as Bruegel the Elder, Rubens, Van Dyck, Jordaens, and Bosch.

Genres: The collection includes paintings, sculptures, decorative arts, and drawings from the Flemish, Dutch, Italian, and French schools.

Museum of Modern Art (Magritte Museum included):

Collection: This part of the Royal Museums is dedicated to modern and contemporary art.

Magritte Museum: Housed within the Museum of Modern Art, it is entirely devoted to the works of surrealist artist René Magritte.

Modern Art: The collection spans the late 18th century to the present day, showcasing works by modern and contemporary artists.

Wiertz Museum:

Focus: Dedicated to the works of the Belgian romantic painter and sculptor Antoine Wiertz.

Highlights: The museum displays Wiertz's monumental and often dramatic paintings, reflecting the Romantic and Symbolist movements.

Meunier Museum:

Focus: Devoted to the works of Constantin Meunier, a Belgian painter and sculptor associated with the social realist movement.

Highlights: The museum showcases Meunier's works depicting industrial and working-class subjects, reflecting the social and industrial changes of the time.

General Information:

Location: The Royal Museums of Fine Arts are located in the heart of Brussels, near the Royal Palace and the Park of Brussels.

Architecture: The museum complex features a blend of architectural styles, and the buildings themselves are notable examples of 19th-century architecture.

Visitor Information:
The museums often host temporary exhibitions, educational programs, and cultural events.
Visitors can explore the diverse collections and gain insights into the evolution of art from the medieval period to contemporary times.

The Royal Museums of Fine Arts of Belgium offer a comprehensive cultural experience, allowing visitors to immerse themselves in the rich artistic heritage of Belgium and beyond. The collections provide a journey through different artistic movements, styles, and periods, making it a must-visit destination for art enthusiasts.

Key Artworks and Artists
Brussels is a city with a rich artistic history and is home to many famous artworks created by renowned artists from different periods. Some of the famous artworks that can be seen in Brussels are -

1. The Adoration of the Magi by Pieter Bruegel the Elder - a painting that showcases the biblical scene of the Adoration of the Magi and is known for its intricate details and innovative composition.

2. The Garden of Earthly Delights by Hieronymus Bosch - is a triptych painting that depicts a surreal

and imaginative interpretation of paradise, earthly pleasures, and hell.

3. The Lamentation of Christ by Rogier van der Weyden - a painting that depicts the scene of Christ's Lamentation, which is known for its emotional intensity and composition.

4. The Son of Man by René Magritte - a painting that is famous for its surreal self-portrait where the artist's face is hidden behind an apple, reflecting the artist's fascination with symbolism and mystery.

5. The Persistence of Memory by Salvador Dalí - a famous painting that depicts melting clocks and is often displayed at the Magritte Museum in Brussels, adding to the surreal ambiance.

6. Plague in an Ancient City by Paul Delvaux - a surreal artwork that depicts enigmatic scenes, often featuring classical architecture and nude figures.

7. The Hunters in the Snow by Pieter Bruegel the Elder - a painting that captures the beauty and harshness of winter, depicting hunters returning to a village.

8. The Death of Marat by Jacques-Louis David - a neoclassical painting that depicts the death of

Jean-Paul Marat during the French Revolution and is known for its political and artistic convictions.

9. The Portrait of Marguerite van Mons by Anthony van Dyck - a portrait that showcases the elegance and charm of its subject.

10. The Barque of Dante by Eugène Delacroix - a painting inspired by Dante's "Inferno" and reflecting Delacroix's romantic and emotive style.

These are just a few examples of the many famous artworks that can be seen in Brussels. The city's museums continue to preserve and showcase works by masters, spanning different periods and artistic movements, making it a must-visit destination for art lovers.

Parc du Cinquantenaire

Parc du Cinquantenaire, also known as Cinquantenaire Park, is a significant public park situated in the European Quarter of Brussels, Belgium. Designed by the Belgian architect Gédéon Bordiau, the park was created in 1880 to commemorate Belgium's 50th anniversary of independence. The park's central monument is the Triumphal Arch, a neoclassical structure at the apex of the park's triangular design. The arch symbolizes Belgium's fight for independence.

The park also houses museums such as the Cinquantenaire Museum and Autoworld, both of which showcase impressive collections of art, historical artifacts, and vintage cars. In addition, the park features meticulously landscaped gardens, tree-lined avenues, and open lawns with symmetrical designs and geometric precision.

The park is also a popular public gathering space for locals and tourists, hosting cultural events, exhibitions, concerts, and festivals throughout the year. Besides offering expansive green spaces for relaxation and picnics, the park features recreational facilities like playgrounds for children, making it an excellent destination for families.

Parc du Cinquantenaire is easily accessible by public transportation and is near several notable institutions. It's not just a historical and cultural landmark but also a picturesque and enjoyable destination for those seeking a blend of greenery, architecture, and cultural experiences in the heart of Brussels.

Mini-Europe

Mini-Europe is a miniature park located in Brussels, Belgium that showcases scaled-down replicas of renowned architectural landmarks and structures found across Europe. The park's main concept is to provide visitors with an educational and entertaining experience, enabling them to explore the diversity of European culture and architecture in a single, compact location.

The miniature replicas are created at a scale of 1:25, offering visitors a sense of the grandeur of the original structures. Mini-Europe features reproductions of famous landmarks, including palaces, castles, bridges, and monuments from various European countries. Each miniature display is accompanied by information about the historical and cultural significance of the original structure.

The park's interactive features, such as buttons and animations, add an engaging and dynamic dimension to the miniature displays. Visitors can press buttons to activate certain features, such as movement in the models or sound effects, enhancing their experience.

The park is set in beautifully landscaped gardens, designed to complement the cultural and natural context of each landmark. Mini-Europe is a family-friendly destination, attracting visitors of all ages, including families, school groups, and tourists. It serves as an educational tool, providing insights into European history, architecture, and cultural diversity, and is a popular destination for school field trips due to its educational focus.

Mini-Europe is easily accessible by public transportation and is often included as part of the Bruparck complex's attractions. The fees to enter Mini-Europe depend on various factors such as age, type of ticket, and special deals. Visitors can often save money by purchasing a family or combination ticket. To find out more about the admission cost and any current deals, visitors can refer to Mini-Europe's website or ask their customer service.

Overall, Mini-Europe is an excellent destination for those interested in exploring the rich cultural heritage of Europe in a condensed and accessible format. The park's attention to detail in the miniature replicas, combined with the interactive features, makes it a popular and engaging destination.

Overview and Attractions

Many attractions in Brussels are worth exploring, such as the Grand Place, Atomium, Manneken Pis,

Cinquantenaire Park, Royal Palace of Brussels, Parc Leopold, European Quarter, Saint-Michel Cathedral, Magritte Museum, Horta Museum, and Mini-Europe.

The Grand Place is a UNESCO World Heritage Site and features opulent guild halls, the Town Hall, and the King's House. The Atomium is a unique and iconic structure representing an iron crystal magnified, while the small bronze statue of Manneken Pis is a cultural symbol known for its playful and irreverent representation. Cinquantenaire Park houses a Triumphal Arch commemorating Belgium's 50th anniversary of independence, along with museums and green spaces.

The European Quarter is home to EU institutions, including the European Parliament and the Berlaymont building. Saint-Michel Cathedral is a Gothic marvel with stunning stained glass windows and intricate architecture. The Magritte Museum showcases a vast collection of surrealist artworks, while the Horta Museum is the former residence of Victor Horta, an Art Nouveau architect, now serving as a museum.

Lastly, Mini-Europe is a miniature park that features scaled-down replicas of famous European landmarks, offering an educational and entertaining experience.

Whether you are interested in exploring the city's grand squares, iconic structures, and museums or indulging in its gastronomic delights, Brussels is a city that seamlessly blends tradition with modernity.

Cultural and Entertainment Venues

Belgian Comic Strip Center

The Belgian Comic Strip Center, located in Brussels, commemorates the rich tradition and artistry of comic strips, a medium in which Belgium has played a pioneering role. The country is renowned for its contributions to the world of comics, with iconic characters like Tintin, the Smurfs, and Lucky Luke. Housed in a former department store designed by Victor Horta, a renowned Art Nouveau architect, the center itself is a masterpiece and an architectural gem. Its walls are adorned with colorful murals showcasing beloved comic characters, creating an immersive and vibrant atmosphere.

The center features extensive exhibits dedicated to famous Belgian comic characters, including the adventures of Tintin by Hergé. Visitors can explore a diverse collection of original comic strip drawings, manuscripts, and memorabilia. Interactive displays and multimedia installations offer an engaging experience for visitors, allowing them to delve into the world of comics. The center often hosts workshops and events, inviting comic enthusiasts to participate in creative activities. In addition, the center includes a specialized library and a bookshop, allowing visitors to explore and purchase a wide range of comic books.

Belgian comics have left an indelible mark on the global comic scene, and the center serves as a hub for preserving and celebrating this cultural legacy. Its exhibitions and contributions have garnered international recognition, attracting comic enthusiasts from around the world. Situated in Brussels, the Belgian Comic Strip Center is conveniently located for visitors exploring the city's cultural attractions and is easily reachable by public transportation. The center offers a captivating journey into the world of Belgian comics, highlighting the country's artistic prowess and its enduring impact on the global comic industry. It provides a delightful experience for comic aficionados and curious visitors alike.

Royal Palace of Brussels

The Royal Palace of Brussels, located at the heart of the city, stands as a majestic symbol of Belgium's monarchy and is an integral part of its rich historical and cultural heritage.

Historically, the palace serves as the official venue for state functions, ceremonies, and official receptions, even though it is not the residence of the Belgian royal family. The original palace dates back to the 18th century, commissioned by Charles of Lorraine, and underwent subsequent renovations and expansions over the years.

The palace showcases a magnificent example of neoclassical architecture, characterized by symmetry, columns, and grandeur. It is surrounded by beautifully landscaped gardens, offering a serene setting.

The Royal Palace hosts official events such as state banquets, ceremonies, and meetings with foreign dignitaries. During the summer months, the palace is open to the public, allowing visitors to explore certain rooms and exhibitions.

The grand staircase, Mirror Room, and Throne Room are all highlights of the palace. The grand staircase features a majestic ascent adorned with intricate decorations, while the Mirror Room is known for its opulent chandeliers, mirrors, and lavish decor. The Throne Room houses the throne of the king and is used for significant ceremonies.

Visitors during the summer opening can take guided tours to explore the palace's interior, learning about its history and the role it plays in official functions. The Royal Palace represents a blend of cultural, historical, and architectural importance, contributing to the identity of Brussels and Belgium as a whole.

The palace's central location in Brussels makes it easily accessible for both tourists and locals, with visitors able to reach it conveniently using public transportation.

Overall, the Royal Palace of Brussels stands as a testament to Belgium's royal history and architectural grandeur, offering both cultural and visual richness to those who explore its splendid halls and gardens.

Brussels City Museum
The Brussels City Museum, also called the Museum of the City of Brussels, is a significant cultural institution that aims to showcase the rich history and heritage of Brussels. It is situated in the iconic

King's House (Maison du Roi) on the Grand Place, one of the city's most well-known buildings.

The museum offers an in-depth exploration of the medieval roots of Brussels and the evolution of the city over the centuries. It houses an extensive collection of artifacts, objects, and memorabilia that provide insights into the daily life, culture, and history of Brussels. Visitors can see scale models of Brussels at different times in history, illustrating the city's growth and architectural changes.

One of the most remarkable exhibits at the museum is the Manneken Pis collection, which showcases various costumes worn by the famous little bronze statue. The collection includes diverse outfits provided by different organizations and countries, providing a unique perspective of the statue's significance to the city.

Another notable exhibit is the giant tapestry map of Brussels, which depicts a detailed representation of the city during the 17th century. The tapestry captures intricate details of the city's streets, landmarks, and buildings, providing visitors with an immersive experience of the city's past.

The museum also has a dedicated room that presents a panoramic view of the Grand Place, allowing visitors to appreciate the architectural splendor of the central square. Interpretative panels provide historical context and details about the buildings surrounding the Grand Place, offering a comprehensive understanding of the city's past.

Being located on the Grand Place, the museum is centrally situated and easily accessible for tourists exploring the heart of Brussels. Visitors can combine a visit to the museum with exploring other cultural and historical landmarks in the vicinity. The museum hosts temporary exhibitions and cultural events, such as lectures, workshops, and cultural programs, making it a cultural hub.

Overall, the Brussels City Museum is an educational and captivating journey through the city's past, providing a comprehensive understanding of Brussels' intricate history and cultural evolution. Beyond its exhibits, the King's House itself is a stunning example of Gothic and Renaissance architecture, making the museum a must-visit for experts interested in the rich heritage of Brussels.

Chapter 4:

Food and Drink

Belgian Chocolate and Waffles
Belgium is synonymous with artisanal chocolate
craftsmanship, maintaining a tradition of excellence
that has elevated Belgian chocolate to
world-renowned status. Chocolatiers in Belgium
take pride in their meticulous approach, using
high-quality cocoa beans and ingredients to create
chocolates of exceptional quality.

Variety of Flavors:
One of the hallmarks of Belgian chocolate is its
diverse range of flavors. Pralines, a type of filled
chocolate, are particularly famous. Chocolatiers
experiment with a myriad of soft or liquid centers,
including ganache, caramel, and nut pastes. Dark,
milk and white chocolates are all expertly crafted,
offering a spectrum of taste experiences.

Chocolatiers and Brands:
Belgium boasts several iconic chocolatiers and
brands that have played a pivotal role in shaping the
global perception of Belgian chocolate. Neuhaus,
established in Brussels in 1857, is credited with
inventing the praline. Godiva, founded in Brussels

in 1926, has become a symbol of luxury and indulgence.

Chocolate Museums:
For enthusiasts keen on delving into the world of Belgian chocolate, museums like Choco-Story in Brussels provide an immersive experience. Visitors can learn about the history of chocolate-making, witness the production process, and indulge in tastings.

Chocolate Festivals:
Belgium hosts chocolate festivals such as Salon du Chocolat, where chocolatiers showcase their creativity. These events offer attendees the opportunity to sample a wide array of chocolates, attend workshops, and appreciate the artistry behind each creation.

Belgian Waffles:
Varieties:
Belgian waffles come in two main varieties, each with its distinct characteristics. Brussels waffles are lighter and crispier, typically served rectangular and adorned with toppings like whipped cream, chocolate, or fruit. On the other hand, Liège waffles are thicker and chewier, featuring sweetened dough with chunks of pearl sugar.

Toppings and Accompaniments:
Both Brussels and Liège waffles are versatile canvases for an array of toppings. Whipped cream, chocolate sauce, and fresh fruits are common accompaniments, providing a delightful blend of textures and flavors.

Street Food Culture:
Waffles are integral to Belgium's street food culture. Street vendors across the country offer these delectable treats, making it easy for locals and visitors alike to enjoy a warm waffle while exploring the charming streets.

Waffle Houses:
Dedicated waffle houses have become institutions, offering extensive menus with various topping combinations. These establishments provide a cozy setting for indulging in the classic Belgian waffle experience.

Cultural Icon:
Belgian waffles have transcended local boundaries to become a global cultural icon. Served in cafes and tearooms, they are cherished for their unique texture and flavor, making them a must-try for anyone exploring Belgian cuisine.

Waffle Festivals:
Wafel Feest (Waffle Festival) and similar events celebrate the beloved waffle. These festivals feature competitions, tastings, and a variety of waffle styles, highlighting the cultural significance of this beloved treat.

Indulging in Belgian chocolate and waffles is not just a culinary experience; it's a cultural journey that captures the essence of Belgium's rich gastronomic heritage.

Recommended Places

Explore the vibrant and culturally rich city of Brussels with these recommended places. From historic squares to iconic landmarks to cultural institutions, each location contributes to the unique tapestry of the city.

Start your journey at the breathtaking Grand Place, a UNESCO World Heritage Site surrounded by opulent guild halls, the Town Hall, and the King's House. Visit in the evening when the square is beautifully illuminated, creating a magical atmosphere.

Marvel at the Atomium, a unique structure representing an iron crystal magnified, built for the 1958 World's Fair. Take an elevator to the top sphere for panoramic views of the city.

Discover the small bronze statue of Manneken Pis, a playful and irreverent symbol of Brussels. Check the statue's wardrobe, as it often sports different costumes provided by various organizations.

Immerse yourself in the world of art at the Royal Museums of Fine Arts of Belgium, housing an extensive collection of paintings, sculptures, and decorative arts. Explore the Magritte Museum dedicated to the works of surrealist artist René Magritte.

Stroll through Parc du Cinquantenaire and admire the Triumphal Arch, commemorating Belgium's 50th anniversary of independence. Explore the museums within the park, including the Autoworld and the Royal Museum of the Armed Forces.

Visit Saint-Michel Cathedral, a stunning Gothic cathedral with intricate stained glass windows. Climb to the top of the tower for panoramic views of Brussels.

Dive into the world of comic art at the Belgian Comic Strip Center, showcasing the country's rich tradition of comic strips. Appreciate the Art Nouveau architecture of the center, designed by Victor Horta.

Explore the Brussels City Museum, housed in the King's House, to learn about the city's medieval origins and cultural evolution. Discover the museum's collection related to the famous Manneken Pis statue.

Enjoy a unique experience at Mini-Europe, featuring scaled-down replicas of famous European landmarks. Engage with interactive displays and learn about the cultural diversity of Europe.

Wander through the Sablon district known for its antique shops, art galleries, and charming cafes. Visit Place du Grand Sablon, a square surrounded by elegant buildings and hosting a weekend antique market.

These recommended places offer a diverse and enriching experience, allowing you to immerse yourself in the history, art, and cultural vibrancy of Brussels.

Belgian Beer
Trappist Beers:
Chimay: Sample beers from Chimay, produced by Trappist monks. The Chimay Blue, in particular, is renowned for its rich and complex flavor profile.

Westvleteren: Seek out Westvleteren, known for limited production and highly sought-after brews, including the Westvleteren 12.

Abbey Beers:
Leffe: Enjoy beers from Leffe, an iconic brand with a range of Abbey beers, including Blonde, Brune, and Tripel.
St. Bernardus: Explore St. Bernardus beers, which have a connection to the Trappist tradition and are celebrated for their quality.

Lambic Beers:
Cantillon: For lambic enthusiasts, Cantillon Brewery in Brussels is a must-visit. Try their traditional sour lambic and gueuze.
Boon Brewery: Boon Brewery is another excellent choice for lambic-style beers, offering a refreshing and tart taste.

Belgian Dubbel, Tripel, and Quadrupel:
Westmalle: Westmalle is renowned for its Dubbel and Tripel Trappist ales, exemplifying the style with robust flavors.
Rochefort: Rochefort offers strong and flavorful Quadrupel ales, known for their complexity and rich malt character.

Belgian Blond Ales:
Duvel: Duvel is a classic Belgian Blond Ale, known for its effervescence and fruity, spicy notes. It's widely available and enjoyed globally.
La Chouffe: La Chouffe is a Belgian Blond Ale with a playful character, featuring a blend of coriander and orange peel.

Belgian Strong Dark Ales:
Gulden Draak: Experience Gulden Draak, a Belgian Strong Dark Ale with a complex flavor profile, including notes of dark fruit, caramel, and chocolate.
Piraat: Piraat is another notable Strong Dark Ale with a robust and warming character.

Witbiers:
Hoegaarden: Hoegaarden is famous for its refreshing Witbier, a Belgian wheat beer brewed with coriander and orange peel.
Celis White: Celis White, originally from Hoegaarden, is a revived classic with a crisp and citrusy profile.

Saisons:
Saison Dupont: Saison Dupont is a classic Belgian saison with a dry and peppery character, making it a refreshing choice.

Brasserie-B Dupont: Explore beers from Brasserie-B Dupont, known for their commitment to traditional saison brewing.

Kriek and Framboise:

Cantillon Kriek: If you enjoy fruit-infused beers, try Cantillon Kriek, a lambic beer aged with cherries, or Cantillon Framboise with raspberries.

Boon Kriek: Boon Brewery's Kriek is another excellent choice for cherry-infused lambics.

Belgian Beer Cafés:

Delirium Café: Visit Delirium Café in Brussels, known for its extensive beer menu featuring a wide variety of Belgian beers.

Moeder Lambic: Moeder Lambic in Brussels and Fontainas in Brussels offer a diverse selection of Belgian craft beers on tap.

Belgian beer is a rich tapestry of diverse styles, each with its unique characteristics and brewing traditions. Whether you're a fan of Trappist ales, Abbey beers, lambics, or other Belgian styles, exploring the country's beer culture is a delightful journey for beer enthusiasts.

Beer Culture Overview

Diverse Beer Styles:

Trappist Ales: Belgium is famous for its Trappist ales, brewed by monks in Trappist monasteries.

Notable examples include beers from Chimay, Westvleteren, and Westmalle.

Abbey Beers: Many Belgian breweries produce Abbey beers, inspired by traditional monastic recipes. Leffe and St. Bernardus are well-known brands in this category.

Lambic and Gueuze: Lambic beers, fermented with wild yeast strains, are the base for Gueuze, a blend of young and aged lambics. Cantillon and Boon Brewery are esteemed lambic producers.

Dubbel, Tripel, and Quadrupel: These strong ales, often associated with Trappist breweries, showcase rich malt flavors. Westmalle and Rochefort are respected for their Dubbel and Tripel styles.

Beer Diversity:

Blond Ales: Duvel and La Chouffe represent the classic Belgian Blond Ale style, characterized by a pale color and a balance of fruity and spicy notes.

Strong Dark Ales: Gulden Draak and Piraat are examples of Belgian Strong Dark Ales, offering a robust and complex flavor profile with dark fruit and caramel notes.

Witbiers: Hoegaarden and Celis White are renowned for their Witbiers, brewed with wheat, coriander, and orange peel, resulting in a refreshing and citrusy beer.

Saisons: Saison Dupont and Brasserie-B Dupont are iconic examples of Belgian saisons, known for their dry and peppery characteristics.

Fruit Beers:
Kriek and Framboise: Cantillon Kriek and Boon Kriek are cherry-infused lambics, while Cantillon Framboise features raspberries, adding fruity and tart elements to the beers.
Innovation: Belgian brewers often experiment with unique ingredients, creating innovative fruit-infused beers and blends.

Glassware and Presentation:
Proper Glassware: Each beer style in Belgium has its designated glassware to enhance the drinking experience. The shape of the glass is designed to highlight the beer's aromas and flavors.
Ritual of Pouring: The ritual of pouring Belgian beers involves a careful pour to create the right amount of foam, which contributes to the overall taste and aroma.

Beer Cafés and Bars:
Café Culture: Belgium is home to a vibrant beer café culture. Establishments like Delirium Café in Brussels and Moeder Lambic offer an extensive selection of Belgian beers on tap.

Tasting Flights: Many beer cafés offer tasting flights, allowing patrons to sample a variety of beers and explore the diverse flavors Belgian beer has to offer.

Beer Tourism:
Brewery Tours: Beer tourism is popular in Belgium, with breweries often welcoming visitors for tours and tastings. The experience allows beer enthusiasts to learn about the brewing process and history of each brewery.

Beer and Food Pairing:
Culinary Experience: Belgian beer culture embraces the concept of beer and food pairing. The diverse flavors of Belgian beers complement a wide range of dishes, enhancing the culinary experience.

Beer Festivals:
Celebrations of Beer: Belgium hosts numerous beer festivals throughout the year, such as the Zythos Beer Festival, where beer lovers can explore a vast array of Belgian beers in a festive atmosphere.

Respect for Tradition:
Preservation of Heritage: Belgian brewers take pride in preserving brewing traditions. Trappist and Abbey breweries, in particular, continue to produce beers following centuries-old methods.

International Recognition:

Global Impact: Belgian beers have achieved global recognition and are celebrated for their quality, diversity, and the cultural significance embedded in each brew.

Belgium's beer culture is a rich tapestry woven with tradition, innovation, and a deep appreciation for diverse flavors. From historic Trappist ales to experimental fruit-infused lambics, Belgian beers offer a journey of exploration and enjoyment for beer enthusiasts around the world.

6.2.2 Popular Breweries and Bars

Belgium is renowned for its rich beer culture that is steeped in tradition, which offers an experience that is unique and unforgettable. To truly appreciate Belgian beer, visitors must explore the breweries and bars that are celebrated for their exceptional craftsmanship and diverse range of styles.

The Chimay Brewery is located in Chimay and is renowned for its Trappist beers, including Chimay Blue, Chimay Red, and Chimay White. The brewery offers guided tours of the brewing facilities and the Chimay Experience, which provides insights into the Trappist brewing traditions.

The Westvleteren Brewery, located in Westvleteren, produces highly sought-after Trappist ales, including Westvleteren 12 (XII), which is often regarded as one of the best beers in the world. However, purchasing beer directly from the monastery requires reservations due to limited availability.

The Westmalle Brewery is located in Westmalle and is known for brewing classic Trappist ales, including Westmalle Dubbel and Westmalle Tripel. The brewery offers tours that provide visitors with a glimpse into the brewing process and Trappist traditions.

The Cantillon Brewery, located in Brussels, is famous for traditional lambic beers, gueuze, and fruit-infused lambics like Kriek and Framboise. The brewery offers guided tours where visitors can witness the spontaneous fermentation process and explore the brewery's history.

The Duvel Moortgat Brewery is located in Puurs and is known for Duvel, a strong and iconic Belgian Blond Ale with a distinctive hop character. The brewery offers tours that provide an in-depth look at the brewing process and include tastings of Duvel and other beers in their portfolio.

In addition to the breweries, Belgium is home to several bars and cafes that are celebrated for their beer selection and ambiance. The Delirium Café, located in Brussels, holds the Guinness World Record for the most varieties of beer available, offering an extensive selection of Belgian and international beers. The Moeder Lambic, located in Brussels, is known for its carefully curated selection of Belgian craft beers on tap, showcasing a range of styles and flavors. The Kulminator, located in Antwerp, is a legendary beer bar known for its extensive cellar, offering a wide array of vintage and rare Belgian beers. 't Brugs Beertje, located in Bruges, is a charming beer bar with a well-curated beer list, including Belgian classics and lesser-known gems. The Dulle Griet, located in Ghent, is known for its impressive beer menu, including the infamous "Max" beer served in a special glass that visitors need to surrender their shoe as collateral to drink. Lastly, the Café Rose Red, located in Bruges, is a cozy café with an extensive selection of Belgian and international beers, known for its intimate atmosphere.

Exploring these breweries and bars offers a comprehensive journey through Belgium's rich beer culture, allowing visitors to savor the craftsmanship and diversity of Belgian beers in iconic settings.

6.3 Local Cuisine

Belgium is renowned for its rich and diverse culinary traditions. Here are some iconic dishes and specialties that represent the heart of Belgian local cuisine:

Moules Frites (Mussels and Fries):
Description: Steamed mussels are often cooked with aromatic ingredients such as garlic, onions, and herbs, and served in a large pot. They are accompanied by crispy golden fries and often enjoyed with a side of mayonnaise.

Popular Variations: Moules Marinières (mussels cooked in white wine, garlic, and herbs) and Moules à la Crème (mussels in a creamy broth) are classic variations.

Belgian Waffles:
Description: Light, fluffy, and slightly crispy, Belgian waffles are a beloved treat. They can be served with a variety of toppings, including powdered sugar, whipped cream, chocolate sauce, fruits, or ice cream.

Varieties: Brussels Waffles (rectangular and lighter) and Liège Waffles (thicker and chewier) are two main types.

Frites (Fries):
Description: Belgian fries are more than just a side dish; they are a cultural phenomenon. They are

typically thick-cut, double-fried to achieve a crispy exterior, and served in a paper cone with various sauces like mayonnaise, ketchup, or aioli.

Friteries: Friteries (fry stands) are common throughout Belgium, offering a quick and tasty snack.

Stoemp:

Description: A hearty and comforting dish, Stoemp is a mashed potato dish mixed with other root vegetables, such as carrots or cabbage. It is often served with sausages or other meats and drizzled with a flavorful sauce.

Carbonnade Flamande (Flemish Beef Stew):

Description: This traditional Belgian stew features beef slow-cooked with onions, brown sugar, and Belgian beer. It results in tender meat with a rich, sweet-savory flavor. It's often served with fries or mashed potatoes.

Waterzooi:

Description: Waterzooi is a creamy soup or stew made with fish or chicken, vegetables, and a broth enriched with cream and egg yolks. It's a specialty of Ghent and is known for its velvety texture and delicate flavor.

Endive Gratin (Gratin d'Endives):

Description: Endive (chicory) is braised and then wrapped in ham before being baked in a creamy béchamel sauce. This dish highlights the balance between the slightly bitter endive and the richness of the sauce.

Speculoos:
Description: Speculoos are spiced, crunchy cookies with a distinct caramelized flavor. They are often enjoyed on their own or used in desserts, and they pair wonderfully with coffee.

Belgian Chocolate:
Description: Belgium is synonymous with high-quality chocolate. Belgian chocolates come in various forms, including pralines, truffles, and bars. They are crafted with precision and are often enjoyed as a sweet treat or a thoughtful gift.

Cheese:
Description: Belgium has a rich cheese tradition. From creamy blues to tangy aged varieties, Belgian cheeses are diverse and often enjoyed with bread, fruits, or as part of a cheese platter.

Liege Gaufre (Liege Waffle):
Description: Liege waffles are a sweet delicacy made from a yeast-based dough with chunks of pearl sugar. They have a denser and chewier texture

compared to Brussels waffles and are often enjoyed plain or with a dusting of powdered sugar.

Belgian cuisine reflects the country's cultural diversity, blending influences from French, Dutch, and German traditions. Exploring these dishes is a delicious way to immerse yourself in the culinary richness of Belgium.

Traditional Dishes

Belgium boasts a rich culinary heritage, and traditional dishes reflect a fusion of French, Dutch, and German influences. Here are some quintessential Belgian dishes that are cherished for their flavors and cultural significance:

Carbonnade Flamande:

Description: A classic Flemish beef stew made with beef, onions, brown sugar, mustard, and Belgian beer. It is slow-cooked to perfection, resulting in tender meat with a sweet-savory flavor.

Waterzooi:

Description: A traditional Belgian fish or chicken stew with vegetables, herbs, and a creamy broth made with egg yolks and cream. It hails from Ghent and offers a comforting and velvety texture.

Stoemp:

Description: Mashed potatoes mixed with vegetables such as carrots, leeks, or cabbage.

Stoemp is often served alongside sausages or other meats, creating a hearty and satisfying dish.

Moules Frites:

Description: Steamed mussels cooked with garlic, onions, and herbs, served with a side of crispy golden fries. It is a beloved dish enjoyed throughout Belgium and often accompanied by various sauces.

Endive Gratin (Gratin d'Endives):

Description: Endive (chicory) is braised, wrapped in ham, and baked in a creamy béchamel sauce. This dish strikes a balance between the slightly bitter endive and the rich sauce.

Vol-au-Vent:

Description: A classic Belgian dish featuring a puff pastry shell filled with a creamy stew, usually made with chicken and mushrooms. It's a hearty and flavorful comfort food.

Paling in 't Groen (Eel in Green Sauce):

Description: Eel cooked in a vibrant green herb sauce made with parsley, sorrel, and other aromatic herbs. It's a specialty often associated with Belgian cuisine, particularly in the region of Brussels.

Chicons au Gratin (Baked Endives):

Description: Endives are wrapped in ham, baked, and topped with a cheesy béchamel sauce. This dish showcases the versatility of endives in Belgian cooking.

Lapin à la Bière (Rabbit in Beer):
Description: Rabbit cooked in beer, often flavored with mustard and aromatic herbs. This dish reflects the Belgian love for incorporating beer into savory recipes.

Filet Américain (Steak Tartare):
Description: Finely chopped raw beef seasoned with onions, capers, Worcestershire sauce, and spices. It is often served with a raw egg yolk on top and accompanied by bread or fries.

Potjevleesch:
Description: A traditional Flemish dish consisting of various meats, such as rabbit, chicken, and veal, cooked in a terrine with a jelly-like broth. It is typically served cold.

Anguilles au Vert (Eels in Green Sauce):
Description: Eels cooked in a green herb sauce made with spinach, sorrel, and other aromatic herbs. This dish is a testament to the country's historical connection with waterways.

Boudin Blanc (White Pudding):
Description: A white sausage made with pork, milk-soaked breadcrumbs, and spices. It is typically pan-fried and served with applesauce.

Tomate aux Crevettes Grises (Tomato with Gray Shrimp):
Description: A simple but delicious dish featuring a hollowed-out tomato filled with tiny North Sea

gray shrimp, often mixed with mayonnaise and herbs.

Speculoos:

Description: Spiced, crunchy cookies with a caramelized flavor. Speculoos are popular as both a standalone treat and as an ingredient in desserts.

Exploring these traditional Belgian dishes provides a glimpse into the country's culinary heritage, showcasing a range of flavors, techniques, and regional specialties.

Recommended Restaurants

Brussels has a vibrant culinary scene with a variety of restaurants offering diverse cuisines. Here are some recommended restaurants in Brussels across different categories:

Belgian Cuisine:

Aux Armes de Bruxelles:

Location: Rue des Bouchers 13, 1000 Brussels

Specialty: Classic Belgian dishes, including Moules Frites and Carbonnade Flamande, served in a traditional brasserie setting.

Belga Queen:

Location: Rue Fossé aux Loups 32, 1000 Brussels

Specialty: Modern Belgian cuisine in a beautifully renovated former bank building. Known for its elegant atmosphere and creative dishes.

Seafood:

Noordzee / Mer du Nord:
Location: Rue Sainte-Catherine 45, 1000 Brussels
Specialty: A seafood bar offering a variety of fresh fish, seafood snacks, and seafood platters. Popular for its casual and lively atmosphere.

International Cuisine:

L'atelier en Ville:
Location: 26 Rue du Vieux Marché aux Grains, 1000 Brussels
Cuisine: French-Belgian fusion with a focus on seasonal and locally-sourced ingredients. Offers a refined dining experience.

Bonsoir Clara:
Location: Rue de Flandre 38, 1000 Brussels
Cuisine: Mediterranean-inspired cuisine with a menu that changes regularly. Known for its cozy ambiance and creative dishes.

Fine Dining:

Comme Chez Soi:
Location: Place Rouppe 23, 1000 Brussels
Cuisine: Michelin-starred restaurant offering French-Belgian cuisine in an elegant setting. Known for its high-quality ingredients and impeccable service.

Bruneau:
Location: Avenue Broustin 73, 1083 Ganshoren

Cuisine: Another Michelin-starred restaurant, Bruneau offers a gourmet experience with a focus on French-Belgian cuisine.

Vegetarian/Vegan:
Humus x Hortense:
Location: 2-4 Rue de Vergnies, 1050 Ixelles
Cuisine: Plant-based restaurant with a focus on seasonal and organic ingredients. Offers creative and flavorful vegetarian and vegan dishes.

Chocolate and Desserts:
Pierre Marcolini:
Location: Galerie de la Reine 24, 1000 Brussels
Specialty: Renowned chocolatier offering high-quality chocolates and pastries. A must-visit for chocolate enthusiasts.
Wittamer:
Location: 12-13-14 Place du Grand Sablon, 1000 Brussels
Specialty: Established patisserie known for its exquisite pastries and desserts. A great place for a sweet indulgence.

These are just a few options, and Brussels has a wide range of restaurants catering to different tastes and preferences. When exploring the city, consider trying both traditional Belgian dishes and exploring the diverse international culinary offerings.

Chapter 5:

Shopping and Day Trips

Shopping Districts and Markets

The city of Brussels boasts several vibrant shopping districts and markets that offer visitors an array of retail experiences. Rue Neuve, situated at Rue Neuve in Brussels, is a bustling pedestrian-friendly street and a hub for fashion, accessories, and cosmetics, featuring an array of international and Belgian brands. Avenue Louise, on the other hand, is an upscale shopping destination, renowned for its luxurious boutiques and designer stores that offer high-end fashion and stylish home decor.

Galeries Royales Saint-Hubert, inaugurated in 1847, is a shopping arcade that is a masterpiece of architecture, housing luxury boutiques, chocolatiers, bookshops, and cafes, and a delight for shoppers. The Grand Place, known primarily as Brussels' central square, hosts a daily flower carpet market during summer. In addition, the surrounding streets are home to a range of souvenir shops and artisanal boutiques.

The Sablon District, situated in Brussels, is a charming area that is renowned for its antique shops, art galleries, and high-end boutiques. Each weekend, the Place du Grand Sablon hosts an antique market that attracts collectors and enthusiasts. The Marolles Flea Market, held daily at Place du Jeu de Balle, is an ideal spot for those seeking unique souvenirs and pre-loved goods, and is a treasure trove of vintage items, antiques, and quirky finds.

The Brussels Design Market, held biannually at Tour & Taxis, Avenue du Port 86C, is Europe's largest vintage design market. The event features mid-century furniture, lighting, and decor items, attracting design enthusiasts' attention. Matongé, situated in Ixelles, is Brussels' African quarter, showcasing a diverse range of shops and markets, from African fabrics to traditional crafts and vibrant street markets that exhibit the area's multicultural character.

Finally, the Flagey Market, which takes place on weekends at Place Flagey, 1050 Ixelles, is known for its lively atmosphere and diverse offerings. It features a mix of food stalls, vintage items, clothing, and handmade crafts. Wolvendaal Flea Market, held on weekends in Wolvendaal Park, 1020 Laeken, is a more relaxed and community-focused market that offers a range of second-hand goods, vintage items, and local crafts.

Local Specialties and Souvenirs

Brussels is renowned for its distinct culture, craftsmanship, and flavors. If you're looking to bring home a piece of the city, consider these unique local specialties and souvenirs:

1. Belgian Chocolate: Belgium is widely known for its high-quality chocolate, particularly pralines, truffles, and artisanal chocolate bars. Notable chocolatiers include Neuhaus, Godiva, and Leonidas.

2. Speculoos: These spiced shortcrust biscuits have a distinct caramelized flavor and are often shaped into windmills or other figures. Speculoos come in various forms, from cookies to spreads.

3. Manneken Pis Souvenirs: Manneken Pis, the iconic bronze statue of a little boy urinating, is a symbol of Brussels. Souvenirs featuring this famous figure include keychains, magnets, and replicas of the statue in various materials.

4. Brussels Lace: Handmade lace items, such as tablecloths, doilies, and handkerchiefs, make for elegant and unique souvenirs. Brussels lace is a traditional craft, so look for specialized lace shops in the city.

5. Atomium-themed Items: The Atomium is a unique building and museum in Brussels, making it an iconic symbol. Souvenirs like miniature Atomium replicas, postcards, and prints capture the spirit of this architectural marvel.

6. Tintin Merchandise: The Adventures of Tintin, created by Belgian cartoonist Hergé, is a beloved comic series. Tintin-themed merchandise, including books, figurines, and posters, can be found in Brussels' comic book shops.

7. Brussels Waffle Mix: Bring home a taste of Brussels' most iconic treats by purchasing a waffle mix. It's a convenient way to recreate the flavor of Brussels waffles at home.

8. Gueuze and Belgian Beer: Belgium is known for its diverse and flavorful beers. Gueuze, a traditional Belgian style of beer, makes for a unique and authentic souvenir. Select a few bottles of Belgian beer to enjoy or share with friends.

9. Comic Books and Graphic Novels: Brussels has a rich comic book heritage, and there are numerous comic book shops in the city. Look for graphic novels, comics, and artwork from famous Belgian artists.

10. Brussels Souvenir Plates: Decorative plates featuring Brussels' landmarks, such as the Atomium or the Grand Place, make for classic souvenirs. These can be displayed as keepsakes or used for decorative purposes.

11. Belgian Lace Shawls: Delicate lace shawls, scarves, or handkerchiefs made with traditional Belgian lace patterns are beautiful and timeless gifts.

12. Miniature Tintin Statues: Miniature statues or figurines of Tintin and his friends can be delightful collectibles for fans of the iconic comic series.

13. Brussels Sprouts-themed Items: Playfully embrace the city's name association with Brussels sprouts. Look for humorous souvenirs like keychains or kitchen items featuring Brussels sprouts.

When selecting souvenirs, consider the recipient's interests and the cultural significance of the item. Whether it's indulging in Belgian sweets, exploring the world of comics, or bringing home a piece of traditional craftsmanship, Brussels offers a diverse array of memorable souvenirs.

Day Trips
Nearby Attractions

Brussels is centrally located in Belgium, making it convenient to explore nearby attractions and cities. Here are some notable places that you can visit within a relatively short distance from Brussels:

Bruges:
Distance from Brussels: Approximately 1 hour by train or car.
Description: Known as the "Venice of the North," Bruges is a charming medieval city with picturesque canals, cobblestone streets, and well-preserved architecture. Explore the Markt Square, visit the Belfry, and enjoy Belgian chocolates at this UNESCO World Heritage site.

Ghent:
Distance from Brussels: Approximately 30 minutes by train or car.
Description: Ghent is a lively city with a rich history. Visit Gravensteen Castle, stroll along the Graslei and Korenlei canals, and marvel at the impressive Saint Bavo's Cathedral. Ghent is known for its vibrant cultural scene and medieval charm.

Antwerp:
Distance from Brussels: Approximately 40 minutes by train or car.

Description: Antwerp is a dynamic city with a thriving arts and fashion scene. Explore the Cathedral of Our Lady, home to works by Rubens, visit the Royal Museum of Fine Arts, and stroll through trendy neighborhoods like Het Zuid.

Waterloo:
Distance from Brussels: Approximately 30 minutes by train or car.
Description: Visit the historic battlefield of Waterloo, where the Battle of Waterloo took place in 1815. Explore the visitor center, climb the Lion's Mound for panoramic views, and gain insights into the events that shaped European history.

Leuven:
Distance from Brussels: Approximately 30 minutes by train or car.
Description: Leuven is a university city with a lively atmosphere. Visit the stunning library of KU Leuven, explore the Old Market Square, and admire the Gothic architecture of the Town Hall. Don't forget to try local beers in one of the many pubs.

Mechelen:
Distance from Brussels: Approximately 25 minutes by train or car.
Description: Mechelen is a hidden gem with a blend of history and culture. Explore St. Rumbold's

Cathedral, visit the Toy Museum, and take a boat tour along the Dyle River. Mechelen offers a quieter, yet captivating, Belgian experience.

Aachen, Germany:
Distance from Brussels: Approximately 1.5 hours by train or car.
Description: Cross the border into Germany to visit Aachen, known for the Aachen Cathedral, a UNESCO World Heritage site. Explore the historic Old Town and discover the cultural heritage of this charming German city.

Lille, France:
Distance from Brussels: Approximately 1 hour by train or car.
Description: Venture into France to explore Lille, a city with Flemish influence. Visit the Grand Place, admire the architecture of Vieille Bourse, and experience the vibrant culture and cuisine of this French city.

Namur:
Distance from Brussels: Approximately 40 minutes by train or car.
Description: Nestled along the Meuse River, Namur is known for its citadel and charming old town. Take a boat cruise on the river, visit the

Felicien Rops Museum, and enjoy the scenic surroundings.

These nearby attractions offer diverse experiences, from medieval cities to historical battlefields, providing an opportunity to explore the rich cultural tapestry of the region surrounding Brussels.

Transportation for Day Trips
Exploring nearby attractions from Brussels on a day trip can be convenient and efficient with various transportation options. Here are some recommended transportation modes for day trips from Brussels:

Train:
Advantages:
Efficient: Belgium has an extensive and efficient train network. Trains are a quick and comfortable way to reach nearby cities like Bruges, Ghent, Antwerp, and more.
Central Stations: Major cities usually have centrally located train stations, making it easy to start your exploration.
Considerations:
Schedules: Check train schedules in advance and consider purchasing tickets online or at the train station.

Car:

Flexibility: Renting a car provides flexibility in your itinerary, allowing you to explore more remote areas or visit multiple attractions in a day.

Comfort: It can be more comfortable, especially if traveling with a group or carrying a lot of luggage.

Considerations:

Traffic: Brussels can have heavy traffic, so plan your departure time accordingly.

Parking: Check parking options and costs in the destination city, especially in city centers.

Bus or Coach Tours:

Advantages:

Guided Tours: Joining a bus or coach tour offers a guided experience with commentary, making it informative and convenient.

Convenience: No need to worry about navigation or driving; simply enjoy the journey.

Considerations:

Fixed Itinerary: Tours may have a fixed itinerary, so if you prefer flexibility, this may not be the best option.

Bike:

Advantages:

Eco-Friendly: Brussels and nearby cities often have bike-friendly routes, providing an eco-friendly and active way to explore.

Local Experience: Biking allows you to experience the surroundings at a more leisurely pace.

Considerations:

Distance: Consider the distance to your destination and your comfort level with cycling.

Weather: Check the weather forecast, especially if you plan to bike longer distances.

Combination of Public Transport:

Advantages:

Versatility: Combine different modes of public transport, such as trains and buses, for a versatile travel experience.

Considerations:

Timetables: Be mindful of timetables and connections between different modes of transport.

Guided Tours by Companies:

Advantages:

Expert Guidance: Opt for guided tours organized by tour companies, offering expert guidance and a hassle-free experience.

Considerations:

Cost: Guided tours may have a higher cost compared to independent travel.

Before embarking on a day trip, check the schedules, availability, and any COVID-19-related travel restrictions. Choose the transportation mode that aligns with your preferences and the nature of your day trip, whether it's a historical city exploration, a scenic adventure, or a cultural excursion.

Events and Festivals

Annual Events

Brussels is a vibrant city that hosts a diverse range of annual events that showcase its cultural diversity, historical richness, and festive spirit. The city's annual events calendar features some prominent events, including the following:

1. Brussels International Film Festival: This festival is a global celebration of filmmaking, attracting industry professionals, cinema enthusiasts, and filmmakers from around the world. It showcases a wide range of international films, highlighting the latest trends and innovations in the world of cinema.

2. Flower Carpet Brussels: Held biennially in the Grand Place, this event is a spectacular display of floral artistry. A vibrant carpet of begonias, covering nearly 1,800 square meters, adorns the central square, creating an intricate design that is breathtaking.

3. Brussels Jazz Festival: The city's jazz aficionados gather to enjoy world-class performances by traditional and contemporary jazz artists at various venues across the city.

4. Brussels Beer Weekend: This event celebrates Belgium's rich beer culture and offers visitors an opportunity to explore the country's diverse beer offerings. It features beer tastings, brewery visits, and beer-related activities.

5. Ommegang Pageant: This historical reenactment takes place in the Grand Place and depicts a medieval pageant in honor of Emperor Charles V. Participants don elaborate costumes, and the event offers a fascinating journey back in time.

6. Fête de l'Iris (Iris Day): A lively festival that celebrates the Brussels-Capital Region, Fête de l'Iris features parades, concerts, and cultural activities. The festivities highlight the city's unity and diversity.

7. Couleur Café Festival: This multicultural music festival brings together artists from various genres, including reggae, hip-hop, and world music. Held in a vibrant setting, Couleur Café attracts music lovers for a weekend of lively performances.

8. Brussels Christmas Market: The Grand Place transforms into a winter wonderland during the festive season, featuring a Christmas tree, enchanting light shows, and wooden chalets offering gifts, crafts, and seasonal treats.

9. Nuit Blanche (White Night): This nocturnal arts festival transforms Brussels into an open-air gallery, showcasing the work of artists and performers through installations, exhibitions, and performances.

10. Brussels Comic Strip Festival: This festival celebrates Belgium's rich comic book heritage, featuring exhibitions, meeting comic book artists, and various themed activities.

11. Brussels Food Truck Festival: This event offers a diverse culinary experience to food enthusiasts, with food trucks serving international cuisines in a relaxed and festive atmosphere.

12. Brussels Marathon: This event attracts professional and amateur runners from around the world, taking them through the city's scenic routes and passing by iconic landmarks.

These annual events contribute to the dynamic and lively atmosphere of Brussels, providing locals and visitors alike with opportunities to immerse themselves in the city's culture, arts, and traditions throughout the year.

Cultural and Music Festivals

Brussels hosts a dynamic array of cultural and music festivals, reflecting the city's diverse and cosmopolitan spirit. Here's a rejuvenated look at some of the noteworthy events:

Brussels Jazz Marathon:

Description: Immerse yourself in the soulful rhythms of jazz during the Brussels Jazz Marathon. This city-wide event brings together talented musicians, offering performances in various jazz styles at iconic venues, creating an unforgettable experience for jazz enthusiasts.

Couleur Café World Music Festival:

Description: Celebrating the world's rich musical tapestry, the Couleur Café Festival is a vibrant fusion of reggae, hip-hop, world, and electronic beats. With multiple stages and a diverse lineup, it transforms Brussels into a global music hub.

Brussels Summer Grooves Festival:

Description: The Brussels Summer Grooves Festival is a rhythmic journey through various music genres, including rock, pop, electronic, and hip-hop. Spread across the city, it brings together international and local artists for a lively summer celebration.

Sonic Visions Electronic Arts Festival:
Description: Sonic Visions explores the intersection of electronic music and digital arts. This forward-thinking festival features live performances, DJ sets, and discussions, providing a platform for cutting-edge artistic expressions and technological innovations.

Brosella Sonic Explorations Festival:
Description: Held against the stunning backdrop of the Atomium, the Brosella Sonic Explorations Festival combines folk and jazz in an innovative blend. The festival showcases both established and emerging artists, offering a unique sonic experience.

Listen! Brussels Soundscapes Festival:
Description: Listen! Brussels Soundscapes Festival delves into the realms of contemporary electronic and experimental music. Audiences can enjoy live performances, DJ sets, and immersive soundscapes, making it a playground for sonic adventurers.

Brussels Global Harmony Festival:
Description: Brussels Global Harmony Festival celebrates the city's multicultural identity through a

rich tapestry of music and cultural performances. It is a vibrant showcase of diversity, fostering cross-cultural understanding and appreciation.

Balkan Beats Rhythms Festival:
Description: Immerse yourself in the energetic rhythms and traditions of the Balkans at the Brussels Balkan Beats Festival. With live music, dance performances, and workshops, it creates a festive atmosphere infused with Eastern European flair.

Brussels Strings Fusion Festival:
Description: The Brussels Strings Fusion Festival brings together the melodic beauty of string instruments with various musical genres. From classical to contemporary, it showcases the versatility of stringed music in a captivating setting.

Ars Musica Avant-Garde Festival:
Description: Ars Musica is an avant-garde music festival pushing the boundaries of classical and modern compositions. It features performances by local and international artists, offering audiences a unique and experimental musical journey.

Brussels Short Film and Sound Festival:
Description: Beyond showcasing short films, this festival places a spotlight on the symbiotic

relationship between visuals and sound. Expect a blend of cinematic storytelling and live music performances, creating a multisensory experience.

Brussels Harmony of Body and Sound Festival:
Description: Combining wellness with cultural experiences, the Brussels Harmony of Body and Sound Festival focuses on yoga and holistic well-being. Live music performances complement the serene atmosphere, creating a day of mindful rejuvenation.

These festivals contribute to Brussels' cultural vibrancy, offering a plethora of musical genres, artistic expressions, and cultural explorations throughout the calendar year.

Chapter 6:

Practical Tips

Language Considerations

Brussels, as the capital of Belgium and the de facto capital of the European Union, is known for its multilingual and multicultural environment. Here are some important language considerations in Brussels:

Official Languages:
Description: Brussels is officially bilingual, with both Dutch and French recognized as official languages. This reflects the bilingual nature of the Brussels-Capital Region. The presence of the European Union institutions also adds English as a widely used language.

Dutch and French Language Divide:
Description: The linguistic divide in Brussels is noticeable, with the northern part primarily Dutch-speaking and the southern part predominantly French-speaking. This linguistic duality is reflected in various aspects of daily life, including signage, government services, and education.

English Proficiency:

Description: Due to the international character of Brussels, English is commonly spoken and understood, especially in areas with a high concentration of expatriates and European Union institutions. Many residents, particularly in service industries, have a good command of English.

Multicultural Population:

Description: Brussels is home to a diverse population, including expatriates, diplomats, and EU officials from around the world. This diversity contributes to the presence of numerous languages and a generally inclusive atmosphere.

Language of Services:

Description: Public services in Brussels are offered in both Dutch and French. However, English is often used in international and business contexts. Visitors and newcomers should familiarize themselves with basic phrases in both Dutch and French.

Education Language Options:

Description: Brussels offers educational institutions that provide instruction in either Dutch or French. International schools, catering to the expatriate community, often offer curricula in English or other languages.

Cultural and Social Events:
Description: Cultural and social events in Brussels may be conducted in various languages, depending on the nature of the event and its audience. Major cultural institutions often provide information in multiple languages.

Language Usage in Business:
Description: In the business and professional environment, English is widely used, especially in international organizations and companies. However, being aware of the linguistic preferences of clients and partners is considered good practice.

Language in Neighborhoods:
Description: Different neighborhoods in Brussels may have a predominant language, reflecting the linguistic diversity of the city. Understanding the linguistic dynamics of the area you are in can enhance your experience.

Language Policy in the European Union:
Description: As the headquarters of the European Union, Brussels plays a central role in EU affairs. The working languages of the EU institutions include English, French, and German, highlighting the city's significance as a multilingual hub.

Understanding the linguistic landscape of Brussels is essential for effective communication and integration. While knowledge of Dutch and French is beneficial, especially for daily interactions, the cosmopolitan nature of the city ensures that English is widely accepted in many situations. Embracing the multilingual environment adds to the richness of the Brussels experience.

Before traveling to Brussels, it's helpful for visitors to be familiar with some basic phrases in the local languages, which are Dutch and French. Additionally, English is widely spoken, especially in tourist areas and business settings. Making an effort to speak a few phrases in Dutch or French can be appreciated by the locals and contribute to a more immersive travel experience.

Here are some basic phrases in Dutch and French that can enhance your experience:

Dutch (Flemish):
1. **Hello:** Hallo
2. **Goodbye:** Tot ziens
3. **Please:** Alsjeblieft (informal) / Alstublieft (formal)
4. **Thank you:** Dank je wel (informal) / Dank u wel (formal)
5. **Yes:** Ja
6. **No:** Nee

7. **Excuse me / Sorry:** Sorry
8. **Do you speak English?:** Spreekt u Engels?
9. **Where is...?:** Waar is...?
10. **How much is this?:** Hoeveel kost dit?

French:

1. **Hello:** Bonjour
2. **Goodbye:** Au revoir
3. **Please:** S'il vous plaît
4. **Thank you:** Merci
5. **Yes:** Oui
6. **No:** Non
7. **Excuse me / Sorry:** Excusez-moi
8. **Do you speak English?:** Parlez-vous anglais?
9. **Where is...?:** Où est...?
10. **How much is this?:** Combien ça coûte?

Currency Information

In Brussels, as in the rest of Belgium, the official currency is the Euro (EUR). Here are some key points about currency and banking in Brussels:

Euro Banknotes and Coins:

- **Denominations:** Euros are available in various denominations of banknotes and coins.

- Banknotes: €5, €10, €20, €50, €100, €200, and €500.
- Coins: 1 cent, 2 cents, 5 cents, 10 cents, 20 cents, 50 cents, €1, and €2.

Currency Exchange:

- **Banks:** Most banks in Brussels offer currency exchange services. Banking hours are typically from Monday to Friday during business hours.
- **Exchange Bureaus:** Exchange bureaus are also available at airports, train stations, and in tourist areas. They may offer competitive rates, but it's advisable to compare rates before exchanging.

ATMs (Automated Teller Machines):

- **Availability:** ATMs are widespread in Brussels and can be found in various locations, including banks, shopping areas, and tourist hotspots.
- **Accepted Cards:** Major credit and debit cards, such as Visa and MasterCard, are widely accepted. Make sure to inform your bank of your travel plans to avoid any issues with card transactions.

Credit Cards:

- **Acceptance:** Credit cards are commonly accepted in hotels, restaurants, shops, and other establishments. However, it's advisable to carry some cash for small purchases or places that may not accept cards.

- **Chip and PIN:** Many transactions in Belgium, including credit card transactions, may require a chip-and-PIN verification.

Traveler's Cheques:

- **Limited Use:** Traveler's cheques are less commonly used in Brussels, and not all establishments may accept them. It's recommended to rely on a combination of cash and cards.

Tipping:

- **Service Charge:** A service charge is often included in bills at restaurants. However, it's customary to leave small change or round up the bill as a tip.
- **Taxis and Services:** Tipping taxi drivers and service providers is appreciated but not mandatory. Rounding up the fare is a common practice.

Safety Tips:

- **Security Measures:** Exercise standard safety precautions, such as safeguarding your belongings and using secure ATMs.
- **Emergency Numbers:** Familiarize yourself with emergency numbers, including those

for your bank and credit card companies, in case you encounter any issues.

Banking Holidays:
Bank Closures: Banks in Brussels, like in many European countries, are closed on weekends and public holidays. Plan your banking transactions accordingly.

Before traveling, check the current exchange rates, inform your bank about your travel dates, and consider carrying a mix of cash and cards for convenience. Additionally, familiarize yourself with any fees or charges associated with currency exchange or ATM withdrawals to make informed financial decisions during your stay in Brussels.

Safety Tips

While Brussels is generally a safe destination, like any other major city, it's essential to be aware of your surroundings and take basic safety precautions. Here are some safety tips for visitors to Brussels:

Stay Informed:
Stay updated on local news and events, especially in the area you are staying.

Be aware of any travel advisories or warnings issued by your country's embassy or consulate.

Public Transportation:
Use reputable and official transportation services.
Keep an eye on your belongings, especially in crowded places like metro stations and buses.

Pickpocketing:
Be cautious in crowded areas, tourist attractions, and public transportation where pickpocketing can occur.
Keep your belongings secure, and use anti-theft accessories like money belts.

Emergency Numbers:
Familiarize yourself with emergency numbers, including local police, ambulance, and your country's embassy or consulate.

ATM Safety:
Use ATMs in well-lit and secure locations.
Shield your PIN while entering it, and be cautious of your surroundings.

Night Safety:
Stick to well-lit and busy areas if you are out at night.

Avoid poorly lit or deserted streets, especially in unfamiliar neighborhoods.

Scams:
Be cautious of common scams, such as fake petitions, distraction tactics, and people claiming to need assistance.
Do not engage with street performers aggressively seeking money.

Cultural Sensitivity:
Respect local customs and cultural norms.
Be aware of your behavior, especially in religious or sacred sites.

Health Precautions:
Carry necessary medications and know the location of medical facilities.
Stay hydrated and be mindful of your health, especially if you have any pre-existing conditions.

Cybersecurity:
Be cautious with public Wi-Fi, especially for accessing sensitive information like online banking.
Keep your devices and data secure with passwords and updates.
Accommodation Safety:
Choose reputable accommodations and lock your doors and windows.

Store valuables in hotel safes.

Local Laws:
Familiarize yourself with local laws and regulations.
Respect the legal drinking age and smoking regulations.

Photography Etiquette:
Ask for permission before photographing people, especially in culturally sensitive or private settings.
Respect restricted photography areas.

Emergency Services:
Know the location of the nearest hospitals, pharmacies, and police stations.
Carry the necessary contact information with you.

Group Safety:
When exploring unfamiliar areas, especially at night, consider traveling in groups.
Inform someone about your plans, especially if going off the beaten path.
By staying vigilant and following these safety tips, you can have an enjoyable and secure experience while exploring the vibrant city of Brussels. Always trust your instincts and seek assistance if you feel uncomfortable or unsure about a situation.

Conclusion:

Brussels, with its blend of history, culture, and modernity, offers a captivating experience for travelers. From iconic landmarks to diverse neighborhoods, the city provides a wealth of exploration opportunities. By navigating the comprehensive travel guide, visitors can make the most of their time in Brussels, embracing its unique charm and cultural richness.

Encouragement for Exploration

Embarking on the journey to explore Brussels is an exciting and enriching experience filled with cultural wonders, historical marvels, and the warmth of a vibrant city. As you set foot in this unique destination, here's some encouragement for your exploration:

Embrace the Diversity:

Brussels is a melting pot of cultures, languages, and traditions. Take this opportunity to immerse yourself in the rich tapestry of diversity that defines the city. From the cobblestone streets of the Grand Place to the trendy neighborhoods like Ixelles and Saint-Gilles, each corner has its own story to tell.

Indulge in Culinary Delights:

Brussels is a haven for food enthusiasts. Don't miss the chance to savor the world-renowned Belgian chocolates and waffles, sample delectable dishes in local eateries, and explore the city's vibrant culinary scene. Whether you're a foodie or a casual diner, Brussels offers a gastronomic adventure that will leave your taste buds delighted.

Wander Through Time and Architecture:
The city's architectural splendors, from the medieval charm of Grand Place to the futuristic allure of Atomium, create a captivating journey through time. Explore the narrow alleyways of the historic center, marvel at Art Nouveau masterpieces, and appreciate the blend of old and new that makes Brussels an architectural gem.

Connect with Locals:
Brussels is not just a city; it's a community of welcoming and friendly people. Strike up conversations with locals, learn a few phrases in Dutch or French, and discover the warmth that defines the city's hospitality. Engaging with the local community will add a personal touch to your exploration.

Immerse Yourself in Festivities:
Whether it's joining a lively music festival, celebrating cultural events, or simply relishing the festive atmosphere in local markets, Brussels offers a plethora of opportunities to join in the merriment.

Embrace the city's dynamic spirit and participate in the festivities that make each visit unique.

Seize the Moment:
Every step you take in Brussels is a chance to create lasting memories. Capture the stunning architecture, savor the flavors, and relish the moments of tranquility in city parks. Whether you're wandering through museums or enjoying a stroll, seize the moment and make your exploration a collection of cherished experiences.

Stay Curious and Open-Minded:
Brussels is a city that encourages curiosity and open-mindedness. Be open to discoveries, hidden gems, and unexpected encounters. Whether it's stumbling upon an art installation, finding a cozy café, or getting lost in the charm of a neighborhood, stay curious and let Brussels reveal its secrets to you.

Safe Travels:
As you embark on your Brussels adventure, prioritize safety while embracing the joy of exploration. Trust your instincts, follow local guidelines, and relish the freedom that comes with discovering a city known for its welcoming embrace.

May your exploration of Brussels be filled with wonder, cultural richness, and a sense of adventure. Safe travels, and may each moment be a treasure in your travel diary!

Printed in Great Britain
by Amazon

39350368R00086